JUST DO YOUR
DREAM!

A 7-Step Guide
to Help You Do
What You
Always Wanted*

*with Stories That Enlighten, Encourage and Inspire

Montrie Rucker Adams

with Dr. Angela Ali

Kathleen,

Your dreams are waiting to come out. Let the world know your gifts. Thank you for your support.

Mattie)

Just Do Your Dream! A 7-Step Guide to Help You Do What You Always Wanted*
*with Stories That Enlighten, Encourage and Inspire

by Montrie Rucker Adams, APR, DTM, MBA

Published by Northland Publishing Company
11811 Shaker Blvd., Suite 414
Cleveland, OH 44120

Scripture quotations are from the King James Version of the Bible.

Cover and interior design: Blackthorn Studio
Photo Credit: Montrie Rucker Adams: Michael Solomon
©2016 by Montrie Rucker Adams, APR, DTM, MBA
All Rights Reserved.

ISBN: 978-0-9761927-9-4

Library of Congress Cataloging-In-Publication Data
Adams, Montrie V. Rucker

Just Do Your Dream! A 7-Step Guide to Help You Do What You Always Wanted/ Montrie Rucker Adams

ISBN 978-0-9761927-9-4
Self Help 2. Inspiration 3. Encouragement 4. Spiritual

DEDICATION

I DEDICATE this book to my mother, Denotra E. Prewitt Rucker. Her love and sacrifices ensured that I would know Christ, the value of education and the importance of creativity and excellence.

My mother was born in Colt, Arkansas, a rural community of enterprising farm families. Though her parents did not attend college, she and her five siblings were encouraged to pursue higher education. My mother graduated from Central State University in 1955 with a degree in home economics and education. She made sure that I knew my value and worth, regardless of outside messages to the contrary. She encouraged curiosity, independence and hard work. My mother often told me that I can do anything if I set my mind to it.

To our children, Tadj and Najah, onto whom her wisdom and work ethic is passed.

THE credit belongs to the man who is actually in the arena,

whose face is marred by dust and sweat and blood;

who strives valiantly;

who errs, who comes short again and again,

because there is no effort without error and shortcoming;

but who does actually strive to do the deeds;

who knows great enthusiasms, the great devotions;

who spends himself in a worthy cause;

who at the best knows in the end the triumph of high achievement,

and who at the worst, if he fails, at least fails while daring greatly,

so that his place shall never be with those cold

and timid souls who neither know victory nor defeat.

—Theodore Roosevelt
Twenty-sixth President of the United States

CONTENTS

Introduction	2
Read This First!	4
What is Your Concorde?	12
How This Book Can Help You: The 7-Part F System	14
Find (and Know) Yourself	16
Part 1—Fear: Do It Afraid	**21**
Nancy Shulins: Fear Took Center Stage	26
Bryan Mattimore: My Three-Step Process to Overcoming	28
Sonja Fisher: Be Open to Transformation	30
Part 2—Family	**33**
Desiree Jefferies: Embrace Your Worth	38
Sandy Stein: Slaying the Green-Eyed Monster	40
Captain Laura: Flying Solo	42
Part 3—Finances	**45**
Laura Pajestka: Understand Your Options	47
Darryl Douglas: Do What Doesn't Cost	49
Captain Laura: Knock on the Side Doors	51

Part 4—Faith 55

Wendy Glidden: My Faith Was Attacked Every Day 58

Brandon Russell: Faith Cannot Be Self-Centered 60

Kimberly Powell: Faith Is All I Have 62

Darah Zeledon: Find a Way 64

Part 5—Focus: Follow One Course Until Successful 67

Jim Stevens: Draw Strength to Stay Focused 74

Diane Randall: You Must Set Boundaries 76

Sandy Stein: Take It Step-by-Step 78

Part 6—Fortitude 80

Matt Shawver: You Must Keep Going 88

Donna W. Hill: A Blind Writer's Journey 90

Jeaninne Kato: Embracing the Journey Alone 93

Part 7—Forgive Past Failures 97

Conclusion 101

7-Part Review 105

Bonus Download 106

Profiles 107

Appendix: Faith 186

Helpful Resources 191

Acknowledgments 195

About the Authors 198

"WHATEVER You Vividly Imagine
Ardently Desire
Sincerely Believe
and
Enthusiastically Act Upon...
Must Inevitably Come to Pass!"[1]

—Paul J. Meyer, founder
Success Motivation Institute

[1]Paul J. Meyer, www.brainyquote.com/search_results.html?q=paul+j+meyer

INTRODUCTION

REMEMBER when you were a child? I do. If I thought I could do something, I believed it. If I thought I was smart, I was. If I thought I could run fast, I could. If I thought everyone loved me, they did.

Then reality hit.

I tried to do something, and it didn't work. I ran as fast as I could, but it wasn't fast enough. I didn't get the A I studied for and I didn't always feel the love.

The voices that said, "I told you so," or "See, you couldn't do it," grew louder than mine. I began to believe they were right.

But one day, after searching deep within and understanding who I am in God, I realized that I was created for a purpose. If I am to live out that purpose, then the dream that God placed within me must be realized.

I hope that within these pages is the encouragement and inspiration you will need to do what you always wanted.

My desire is that you will find, within the words of over forty success stories, the little nudge you may need to move just one step forward. Read them. Learn from them. Find strength in them.

Jaladduin Rumi, the great 13th Century poet wrote:

"You were born with potential.
You were born with goodness and trust. You were born with ideals and dreams. You were born with greatness.
You were born with wings.
You are not meant for crawling, so don't.
You have wings.
Learn to use them and fly."

JUST DO YOUR DREAM.

READ this FIRST!

THERE was a lot of chatter in the line as we waited to hear the words, "Is everybody ready?" I chimed in a little with the other ladies, if only to relieve my nerves and take my mind off what I was about to do. After training for over a year, I could not believe that what I had longed to do for so many years was about to happen.

The auditorium was packed. People cheered and gave kudos to the competitors who struck their practiced poses. I couldn't help but think, *What am I doing here?*

When the competitors and I finally stood in front of the judges, I was grateful the lights were beaming brightly. They prevented me from seeing the audience. But I could hear the sounds.

"Don't you dare shake on me!" I said to my legs as I struck the poses for the judges and held them until we were told to move. *I'm glad I practiced posing in these five-inch heels!*

"Number 85..." Did I hear that right? Never had I imagined that I would place in the top five. I wanted to win—at least that's what I told myself—but deep inside I didn't think I had a chance. I had already accomplished my goal: To compete. That was enough. *But to win third place?*

Since I had been twenty-five years old, I had a dream to compete in a bodybuilding/figure contest...

MARCH 31, 2012, WAS THE DAY
I ACCOMPLISHED THAT DREAM.

IN 2010, I celebrated my company's tenth anniversary with a fundraiser and dinner. I named the event Don't Drop the Dream and invited clients, friends, and supporters to help me celebrate Visibility Marketing Inc.'s milestone. I wanted to impress on everyone that if a ten-year-old African-American girl from East Cleveland, Ohio, who had been raised by a divorced single mother, could celebrate ten successful years of business ownership, having never "dropped the dream," then they could realize their dreams, too.

I have since changed the slogan to *Just Do Your Dream!* and expanded to include a website (JustDoYourDream.com), a Facebook community, an e-newsletter, and a growing social media presence.

My vision is to see a movement of motivated individuals doing what gives them joy. I want others to step out in faith and do what might initially be fearful, but will ultimately give them satisfaction.

You may have chosen this book because something about the title piqued your curiosity. *Hmm... How to do what I've always wanted. This is exactly what I need,* is what you may have thought.

If you are like me and have a dream deep inside you—something you've always wanted to do (but fear, finances, or family has held you back), this guide will help you overcome whatever it is that stands between you and your dream.

If you happen to be an over-forty-something who has been side-tracked on the way to your dream, this book is for you. Maybe you've had a dream since your childhood, or as a young adult, that hasn't been realized. Now, you may feel as though it's too late.

KNOW THIS... IT'S NEVER TOO LATE TO JUST DO YOUR DREAM!

Oh, yes it is! You may think. *I wanted to be a dancer. Now I can barely walk!* Well, maybe it is too late for you to dance with the Rockettes, the Alvin Ailey Dance Theater, or the San Jose Ballet, but it's never too late for you to dance.

Never.

Iris Hirsch always wanted to be a singer. She married young, and her path went in a different direction. Now, at sixty, she is the lead singer for two bands—the Retro-Rockets and Rearview Mirror. She now performs more than two hundred shows a year in the Columbia, Maryland, area.

It's *never* too late.

After a successful career in business, Peter Barber's childhood love for cheetahs led him from his home in British Columbia, Canada, to Kenya, West Africa. He wanted to spend time living with and helping the animals he had dreamed about as a child.

It's *never* too late.

"You will be a doctor or lawyer," is what Dr. Marisa Silver's parents told her. However, Marisa had a love for the performing arts, which she cultivated in high school. Marisa's dream was different from her parents' expectations. She did become a doctor, but she has also appeared in commercials, on stage, and reality shows.

IT'S NEVER TOO LATE.

When I was ten years old, I decided that I wanted to own a business. On several occasions, I had accompanied my father to his business during my visits to Puerto Rico. There was something special about what I saw in my father as he led his organization. He had a boldness and determination about him. He walked and talked with an aura of confidence that was even evident to a child. I knew one day I would own a business.

My dream was to be a business owner.

Fast-forward nine years. I broke my leg and needed to attend the Cleveland Clinic's Sports Therapy Department for rehabilitation. While on the quadriceps machine, (it strengthens the thigh muscles), I decided to try out the other fitness equipment. From that point on, whenever I attended the rehabilitation sessions, I also made sure to get a full body workout. By age twenty, I was a full-fledged gym junkie.

My dream was to compete as a body builder.

During my middle school years, I established a love for writing. In high school, I entered numerous essay contests and wrote pieces for extra-credit. I won scholarships for my thoughts and my gift of putting pen to paper.

My dream was to be an author.

Now, more than thirty-five years later, I have accomplished all my dreams. I competed in fitness competitions. I am a writer. I am a business owner. However, it took much time and effort for me to finally do what I've always wanted.

Your life's clock is ticking. Have you done what *you've* always wanted?

Remember when you were a child. . .

What did you want to be when you grew up?

Remember what you wanted to do when you graduated high school?

You wanted to impact your community. Did you?

You said you were going to write a bestseller. Did you?

After college. . . ?

Think about it. Or, *have* you been thinking about it for a while now? If so, then it's time to *do* something. If that "thing" you've always wanted to do for the past twenty, thirty, or forty years has been nagging you, calling your name, and poking you in your sleep, it's time to act. I don't believe that God put your dreams within you to remain dormant.

IT'S TIME TO JUST DO YOUR DREAM!

Do you have an itch that needs to be scratched? Have you been talking about it and talking about it, but you've never put one leg in front of the other? Have you started something, but then put it on the back-burner of your mind?

Think about how you will feel once you've scratched that itch. Better yet, think about what it will feel like to realize your dream. When the box next to your dream is checked, you can exhale and relax. You will have finally done it!

This book will...

★ give you tips and pointers, examples, and most of all, the *encouragement* and *inspiration* to place check marks next to your dreams.

★ explore the three things that may be holding you back

★ delve into the four that will propel you forward.

★ introduce you to people who have been where you are, but figured out how to move past the paralysis. They overcame many of the same obstacles that stand in the way of *your* dream. They did it, and so can you!

Just Do Your Dream! is not a "bucket list" book. It's a positive, inspirational guide toward realizing a long-held dream. It's a step-by-step guide to getting it done. It will show you what obstacles you may face and offer suggestions on how to overcome them. In the end, you will feel what I felt after third place in my first fitness contest: *Excited. Accomplished. Relieved.*

Several unfulfilled dreams have plagued me over the years. Writing this book is one of them. If, after more than thirty years, I can put a check mark next to the line that says, "write a book," then you can grab your pen and get ready to make your mark, too!

Before you pick up that pen, I want to introduce you to my friend, Imado.

You may have already met him. He's the guy who shows up when something needs to be done.

When somebody asks when you are going to run your next marathon, what do you say? "Imado it."

"Hey Paul, when are you going to. . ."

"Imado it."

"Cherie, what happened to going back to school? You've been talking about it for a while."

"Imado it!"

Imado doesn't often follow through. What Imado says is not always what Imado does.

So. . . what are *you* going to do?

WHAT IS YOUR CONCORDE?

JAMES McCarthy Prewitt, or "Uncle Mac" as he was called, enjoyed traveling. When he retired from NASA in Cleveland, Ohio, after thirty-five years, he spent twenty years traveling the world. He cruised the Pacific and Atlantic Oceans and the Mediterranean Sea. He flew all over the globe. If a plane, train, or automobile could get him there, Uncle Mac went.

Not bad for an old country boy from Colt, Arkansas, who was born in 1910.

Uncle Mac always talked about flying on the Concorde. He was fascinated by the turbojet-powered supersonic airplane. Many conversations took place in which he mentioned taking a trip on the Concorde.

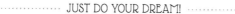

Uncle Mac died on November 16, 2001 at age ninety-one, the same day I gave birth to Tadj Josiah. It was surreal. We were in the same hospital. As Uncle Mac's spirit was leaving us, my son's was arriving.

At the funeral, I looked at Uncle Mac and thought, *He never had the chance to ride the Concorde.*

What is your Concorde? What is it that you've always wanted to do but haven't?

WHAT IS YOUR DREAM?

HOW THIS BOOK CAN HELP YOU— THE 7-PART F SYSTEM

"Everyone has a plan [dream] until they get punched in the face."[2]

—Mike Tyson, former heavyweight champion

I understand that stepping out to do something you've been thinking and probably talking about for a long time can be hard. It's the reason this book is set up like a "blueprint" to help you accomplish your goals. I call it the 7-Part F System.

There are three Fs that can *hinder* you from accomplishing your dreams: fear (the most prevalent of the three), finances, and family.

Then there are four Fs that can *help* you accomplish your goals: faith, focus, fortitude, and forgiveness.

[2] Mike Tyson, www.brainyquote.com/search_results.html?q=mike+tyson

Because I care about you and want to help you "just do your dream, I've also included bonus Fs, beginning with finding yourself and then eventually experiencing the freedom of flourishing.

I promise, if you follow what's in this book, you will accomplish what you set out to do. I'm not promising that it will be easy. Nothing worth having ever is. But what I *will* promise is that you will feel a sense of accomplishment when you finally. . . Just do your dream!

Time marches on. When you first dreamed of climbing one of the world's highest mountains, you were young and ready to take on the world. Now it's twenty (or more) years later. The world is still here waiting.

What are *you* waiting for? Just do you dream. Now.

The tips and guidelines you will read in this book have been proven to work. How do I know? I tried them at least three times, and all three times they worked for me. That's a 100 percent success rate!

So. . .stop wondering. Start doing. That itch? It will go away, and you will experience amazing feelings, too. Excited. Accomplished. Relieved.

JUST DO YOUR DREAM.

FIND (AND KNOW) YOURSELF

"IF you cannot find the truth within yourself, where else do you expect to find it?"[3]

—Dōgen, Thirteenth Century Zen Master

Before we begin Chapter 1, let's talk about *you*. In the words of that famous song by The Who: "Who are you?" Do you know who *you* are? Do you *really* know who you are?

This is an important question to answer. You can't "do your dream" if you don't know *you*. If you can't describe who you are with confidence, then you have some soul-searching to do.

I asked my friend, Cynthia Gilchrist, a certified Career Development Facilitator, her thoughts about fulfilling dreams.

"When a person realizes who they are—their purpose—they instinctively know that they can live nothing less. It wakes up our

[3]Dogen, www.brainyquote.com/quotes/authors/d/dōgen.html

inherent springboard that launches us into our 'drive mode.' We are no longer suffering from the agonizing and tormented feeling that we are supposed to be doing 'something', but just don't know what it is. It's the search for our true, authentic self. Only our authentic self can give birth to our dream(s)."

Cynthia's clients include high school and college students, as well as adults seeking their passions and in some cases, a life career that is an extension of their authentic self.

What do you enjoy doing? What is your gift? How do you like to express yourself? What are you good at that you've never been taught or trained to do? The answers to these questions can help you determine who you really are.

"Many people don't take the time to get to know themselves well," says Dr. Angela Ali, Ph.D., founder of e|volve, a Chicago-based counseling, coaching, and consulting practice. "Knowing who you are opens the door to the things that are important to you, such as personal freedom, social causes, autonomy, creativity, problem solving, helping others, self-advocacy, goal achievement, etcetera," says Dr. Ali. If you want to increase your self-awareness, there are personal inventory assessments that can help you to determine your interests, skills, and abilities.

Dr. Ali adds, "People can get to know themselves better by engaging

in mindfulness, journaling, taking personality and skills assessments, and requesting feedback from others. Mentors, teachers, loved ones, and friends who know you well can often see qualities and characteristics, and weaknesses that you may overlook within yourself. Understanding yourself fortifies *your* position because you become more aware of your strengths, and you can pinpoint areas for growth."

"Ask yourself: *What drives me?* Or, *What am I passionate about?*" says Dr. Ali. "Analyze your lifestyle. Taking the time to understand yourself better, prior to pursuing your dreams, can help you honestly discover any limitations or fears you have, and thus prepare you to make the personal and professional adjustments necessary for success."

L IVING fearlessly is not the same thing as never being afraid. It's good to be afraid occasionally. Fear is a great teacher. What's not good is living in fear, allowing fear to dictate your choices, allowing fear to define who you are. Living fearlessly means standing up to fear, taking its measure, refusing to let it shape and define your life. Living fearlessly means taking risks, taking gambles, not playing it safe. It means refusing to take "no" for an answer when you are sure that the answer should have been "yes." It means refusing to settle for less than what is your due, what is your right, what is yours by the sweat of your labor and your effort.[4]

—Michael Ignatieff, former leader of the
Liberal Party of Canada

[4]Michael Ignatieff, www.obsessedwithmotivation.com/top-10-powerful-quotes-on-being-fearless/

PART 1—FEAR

DO IT AFRAID

"YOU block your dream when you allow your fear to grow bigger than your faith."

—Anonymous

Fear. Is. Real.

In his 1964 book *Faith against Life's Storms*, Oral Roberts, who was an American Methodist-Pentecostal televangelist and founder of Oral Roberts University, writes: "Fear is the most wasting, tormenting, torturing, destroying power known to the human family. Nothing has plowed such furrows, cut such swaths or wrought such havoc as fear. It is the sorrow of man and the ruination of his life."[5]

He continues, "Fear is a false philosophy. It is like a man saying, 'Here

[5]Oral Roberts, *Faith Against Life's Storms*, (Oral Roberts, 1957, 1964), 26.

are the plans for my life. If these plans do not work...well, what is the use? There is nothing else I can do.'"[6]

Fear can stop you from doing. Once you know yourself and start moving forward, fear can stop you dead in your tracks.

Christian author and teacher Joyce Meyer writes in her book, *Do It Afraid*, about how fear is not what God wants for us. We cannot live the lives He intended for us if we are afraid.

Fear controlled me for over twenty-five years until I accomplished my dream of competing in a bodybuilding competition. Many years before the competition, I had surgery, which resulted in a longer-than-fifteen-inch scar on my left leg. *I can't get out there and compete with this ugly scar,* I thought. *And that little itty-bitty skimpy outfit? I'm supposed to get on stage wearing that? Oh no! I'm the one who wears two and three cover-ups at the pool!*

Fear kept me from starting my full-time public relations business sooner than I did. I knew I was going to do it someday, I just didn't know when...or how. I kept putting it off. "I don't have enough experience." "I need *more* credentials..." And putting it off...until I was finally downsized in 2004 from a job that I enjoyed. *I guess I have to start my business now. I'm unemployed!*

Fear kept me from realizing my writing goals, even though my desire to write a book began in high school. My love for novels steered me in the direction of fiction. I signed up for writing workshops, attended writing conferences, and even took many novel writing courses. However, "life" and a paralyzing fear got in the way, and my original manuscripts were shelved.

[6]Ibid., 26.

I played it safe throughout the years and wrote for *Kaleidoscope Magazine*, a local publication that allowed me to interview people and satisfy my writing urges.

In 2010, to combat my fear, I stuck my toe into somewhat deeper waters and wrote *Be More Visible! Create More Interest in You, Your Product or Service*. It's a booklet with tips for business owners and professionals on how to be more visible. It's. . . how many years later? Now, I'm finally attempting to complete a full-scale book.

Think about all the things you could have done but didn't because you were afraid. Maybe you didn't go on that trip with everyone else. When they came back, they told of the wonderful scenery and all the fun they experienced. But you didn't go, so you missed out.

Wait. That's my story.

One summer, my father offered two of my sisters, Terri and Tonia, and me a free trip to Europe. We would look in a thick *Fodor's Travel Guide* and find a place to stay, like a hostel or dorm, and just backpack it. *No way!* I thought. *I am not going to some foreign land and just wander around.* This was the early eighties, so there were no cell phones or Internet, and we would have little contact with friends and family. I decided to not go.

When my sisters returned telling of their journey and the fun they had, I could have kicked myself. I came up with any excuse you could possibly imagine as to why I didn't go, but the real reason was fear.

I'm afraid of many things. . . like flying. But I still fly. I have to if I want to travel and see the world. I say my prayers and ask God to keep us all safe, but I don't allow my fears to stop me. If I did, I would never have visited the West African countries of Ghana, Mali, Côte d'Ivoire,

Japan, Hong Kong, the Caribbean, and many cities in the U.S. I have such wonderful memories now because I chose to get on the plane. I did it afraid.

Most of us are not fully aware of the reasons for our fear. "It can be lonely at the top," says Dr. Ali. "Many people's biggest fear is that they will have a lonely existence if they don't think or do things like the masses. Often people will minimize their talents, abilities, and accomplishments and won't soar because they may lose or outgrow the people around them." However, the cost of not living out one's purpose is equally, if not more, emotionally difficult.

I love the following quote on fear from Dr. Marianne Williamson, spiritual teacher, author, and lecturer. You've seen it in some form, but it's worth repeating here:

> *Our deepest fear is not that we are inadequate. Our deepest fear is that we are powerful beyond measure. It is our light, not our darkness that most frightens us. We ask ourselves, 'Who am I to be brilliant, gorgeous, talented, fabulous?'*
>
> *Actually, who are you not to be? You are a child of God. Your playing small does not serve the world. There is nothing enlightened about shrinking so that other people won't feel insecure around you. We are all meant to shine, as children do. We were born to make manifest the glory of God that is within us. It's not just in some of us; it's in everyone. And as we let our own light shine, we unconsciously give other people permission to do the same. As we are liberated from our own fear, our presence automatically liberates others.[7]*

[7]Marianne Williamson, *A Return to Love: Reflections on the Principles of a "Course in Miracles"* (Harper Collins, 1992), 190. www.en.wikiquote.org/wiki/Marianne_Williamson

"Whether someone has a fear of success or failure, it all boils down to one's fear of discomfort," says Dr. Ali. "The pursuit of any dream or goal will present you with challenges, yet those challenges are what builds the resilience necessary to maintain strength and perseverance while moving in the direction of fulfilling your dreams."

"We are socialized to fear discomfort," says Dr. Ali, "therefore, people will avoid it at all costs in order to *feel good*.'We fill ourselves up with things that distract us from discomfort, such as food, alcohol, denial, unfulfilling relationships, drugs, sex When we use these things to numb the feeling of loneliness, embarrassment, failure, or not being enough, we don't allow the discomfort to inform us about what direction we need to take next in fulfilling our dreams," she explains.

"Don't let fear of failure discourage you. Don't let the voice of critics paralyze you—whether that voice comes from the outside or the inside."[8]

—Dieter F. Uchtdorf, airline executive and religious leader
(LDS Church)

[8]Dieter F. Uchtdorf, *The Remarkable Soul of a Woman* (Salt Lake City, UT: Deseret Book Company, 2010), 15.

NANCY SHULINS' STORY–
FEAR TOOK CENTER STAGE

NOT only did fear play a starring role in my journey from conception to realization of my dream, it was also, at various times, a supporting actor, a featured player, a walk-on, and a cameo. Fear was my Alpha and Omega, my not-so-silent partner, my raison d'être, my plus-one. Yet even as it shadowed me, it also propelled me forward, giving me something to push back against as I baby-stepped my way through the alien universe of horses and the women who love them.

There was no shortage of things to fear. Injuries—my own as well as my hot-blooded young thoroughbreds—were just the beginning. I also feared looking like the rank beginner that I, in fact, was. I was ter-rified of losing my composure while being screamed at by a succession of sadistic trainers (an every-other-day occurrence) and afraid of trying the patience of the far more experienced boarders at my barn. For a very long time, it seemed that, on the rare occasions I attained a modicum of self-confidence, someone—or something—would quickly cut me back down to size.

What made me move forward? My horse. My beautiful horse and the remarkable bond that developed between us, despite my anxieties, despite my mistakes. Had it been only me—me and a snowboard; me and a kayak, me and a hang glider—I may very well have let fear defeat me. But, Eli and I were in this together. What I couldn't do for myself, I did for him.

Nancy found an anchor. She had something to hold on to, something that gave her a reason to move forward and ignore the fear that would sometimes consume her.

When fear steps in, find your anchor. Your anchor could be your children, your spouse, the desire to complete what you started, or merely relishing in the beauty of the dream you so desire.

BRYAN MATTIMORE'S STORY– MY THREE-STEP PROCESS TO OVERCOMING

I'M an introvert. And so the prospect of facilitating idea-generation groups, moderating focus groups, leading creative-thinking workshops, and giving keynote speeches was somewhat terrifying.

I knew that this fear would prevent me from manifesting my mission to popularize the structure of creativity, so I very consciously began a program to help me get beyond this fear. I also knew, from my psychology training at Dartmouth, that it made sense to progressively desensitize myself to this fear. . . to start slow and build up to addressing increasingly fearful situations.

So, I first practiced giving short "talks" in supportive and/or low-risk environments. For instance, I would experiment with "presenting" my ideas on creative thinking with friends and family. I also forced myself to take a philosophy class in college where I knew I would have to give oral presentations.

Secondly, I forced myself to get some training. I enrolled in an adult acting class, an improvisation class, and a stand-up comedy class. Each class was scarier than the last. All three forced me to confront my fear of looking foolish in front of a group.

Finally, I learned and practiced a series of spiritual disciplines to help me relax, become more self-aware, ultimately embrace and yes, even enjoy was what I was doing. These spiritual disciplines included: meditation, contemplation, re-birthing, and soul travel.

And I'm happy to say this program worked. In my career, I have led more than 1,000 group idea-generation sessions, moderated more than 500 focus groups, and given more than 200 keynote speeches. And I LOVE what I do.

Bryan understood his limitations and took the necessary steps toward improvement. As mentioned earlier, this road is not easy. But it's absolutely doable.

What classes can you take?... Which self-help measures can you explore to help you overcome? You can take control of your fear. Don't let it control you.

SONJA FISHER'S STORY–
BE OPEN TO TRANSFORMATION

WHENEVER you have big dreams, you will always face several types of fear, including fear of failure, fear of execution, fear of change, and fear of success.

If you truly are invested in chasing your dreams, you have to be vulnerable and open to transformation, which can be a very scary place. I have faced much fear in going for my dreams, some of which included working on General Hospital, becoming a national pageant winner, earning a doctorate in business, and making a difference for women in technology, business, and entertainment with my own business and initiatives.

Some of the fears I have had to face in my own transformation include finances, putting myself out there, receiving constant rejection, moving away from Minnesota (which I called home for most of my life), sacrificing time with my family and friends, failing health, and putting myself in uncomfortable situations. However, by working through all these fears, I have been able to accomplish so many of my dreams through persevering.

I have worked on General Hospital, was Mrs. Corporate America from 2009–2010, and earned my doctorate in business in 2013. I have been making a difference in women's lives by inspiring them to go for their dreams in technology, entertainment, and business through my new company, Nonstop 4 the Top.

Anything is possible if you put your mind to it and work through your fears to accomplish your life goals! You only live once, so start taking the steps you need to see your dreams be fulfilled!

Sonya understood that in order to realize her dreams, she had to do something different—something she was not accustomed to doing. She stepped out and worked through her fears because her desire to succeed was just that great.

Was there a time when your desire for something was so great that you didn't even recognize any fears you may have had? Fear may have been there, but you knew that what you wanted was greater than the fear that may have prevented you from getting it?

PART 2-FAMILY

"FAMILY is supposed to be our safe haven. Very often it's the place where we find the deepest heartache."[9]

—Iyanla Vanzant, spiritual teacher, author

F-A-M-I-L-Y. This six-letter word is all-powerful. It encompasses the people who know and love us, and the people we know and love.

It's been said that, "Some of the most poisonous people come disguised as friends and family."

It is within this bond of familiarity and love that we are often brought to confusion. When our loved ones seem to contradict themselves— by not supporting our dreams—we're thrown off-kilter, unable to make sense of their actions or behavior.

What do you do when your spouse does not embrace your dream?

[9]Iyanla Vanzant, www.azquotes.com/quote/837081

How do you respond when your parents don't support your passion? How do you relate to those who claim to love you but seem to do all they can to discourage you from moving forward with your goals and purpose?

Some adults move through life deterred, because as children they were teased or discouraged from doing certain things—especially the things they love. They may have heard comments from parents and other family members like: "That's not a field for girls." "You can't do that." "That's crazy!" "Do you think that's a wise choice? You're not smart enough."

Sometimes our family members can be dream killers.

"At times, family members may frown upon our dreams or goals. We may receive negative vibes once we share our plans with them, but often it is because they have fears that you don't. They may feel as though it's impossible to accomplish your dream and are afraid that you'll fail without a backup plan. They may feel that you have a track record of not meeting your goals," says Dr. Ali. "In these cases, they may not provide you with the encouragement you want and need. You can still appreciate the honesty and advice of others regardless of whether it's positive or negative, but refrain from trying to convince others why your dreams are worth pursuing. It's not their job to see the value in your dreams, it's yours.

"You must figure out a way to tune out the naysayers, yet also be able to carefully filter any constructive feedback from those you know have your best interests at heart. This is often a fine line to determine, because in the end, you have to know when useful advice is being given," says Dr. Ali. Remember, it's not *their* dream; it's *yours*.

For instance, Mélanie Hope's parents, teachers, and ex-husband said her dream of travelling and being a professional speaker and published author was "silly." Most of her life was spent in her career working as an accountant. She wanted to become an author and speaker but was told she "didn't matter" and "no one would listen."

When he was seven-years-old, Jim Stevens told his father he wanted to be an artist and a writer. His father responded with a whack on the head followed by, "No son of mine is going to grow up starving in an attic."

Then there's Sandy Stein, whose husband was jealous of her dream. So much so, that he tried to derail it. It was a setback for Sandy, but when you're determined, even dream killers can't disrupt the path to your dreams.

How do you react when the people closest to you, those who should have your best interests at heart, are the very ones who end up sabotaging your dream?

"No one can sabotage your dream," says Dr. Ali. "As the saying goes, 'It's lonely at the top.' If you are the cream that rises to the top of your community, family, and friends, inevitably you will bring *them* face-to-face with their own sense of failure or their own inability to take risks. It's not your fault.

"The bottom line is that everybody can't make the climb. Don't expect everybody to '*get*' you or support you. It doesn't mean they don't love you, but certain relationships may change. You may not be able to spend as much time with family and friends, because chasing your dream will lead you to other people and new places. And that may just make those around you uncomfortable."

Ahh. . . the fear of others' successes.

When people reach for their dreams, it's important that they know and understand that others around them could change. To lessen this "discomfort," they often minimize who they are. Doing so will affect their growth.

When moving in a positive direction, don't ever assume that people won't change around you. They may judge you or not appreciate what you are trying to accomplish. They may expect you to stay the same. But you can't.

"You may even have to keep your dreams to yourself and share only with those who can handle the information. No one can sabotage your dream without your permission," adds Dr. Ali.

"When pursuing your dreams, it's important that you are emotionally mature enough to anticipate changes in both yourself and others. You may even fear 'rising above' others and the inevitable changes it will have on your relationships. Your need to 'rise' may bring others face-to-face with their own sense of failure or unwillingness to take risks. It's not your fault. Others may wonder. . . 'Will you still be there for me when you achieve your future goals? Or will you not be a part of my life anymore?' Understanding others' fears and having compassion for them may be important; however, you want to avoid playing down your achievements or giving up altogether."

Dr. Ali adds, "You may be the cream that begins to rise to the top of your community, family, or friends. The truth is that everybody can't make the climb with you. Don't expect for everyone to 'get' you, or to support your dreams. It doesn't mean they don't love you; but be realistic about the fact that your relationships may change. You may not be able to spend as much time with friends and family while pursuing your dreams, and/or you may spend more time with others with whom they are unfamiliar. The changes they see and experience may make them feel uncomfortable. Unexpectedly, they may fear your success, and this may catch you off-guard."

"I cannot emphasize this enough...," Dr. Ali continues. "When you move in a positive direction, certain people around you will change. So will you. Some people will show up as your best cheerleaders, while others may not appreciate what you are trying to accomplish. They may harshly judge your decisions and actions."

Though we are human, and we are designed to feel connected, our dreams are usually an individual pursuit. As the saying goes, 'It's lonely at the top.'

"This is also where you must get comfortable," Dr. Ali emphasizes. "Feeling alone at times along your journey may take you in a different direction, one that family and friends may not completely understand."

DESIREE JEFFERIES' STORY– EMBRACE YOUR WORTH

I THOUGHT that when I said "I do," I would have someone in my corner for life, helping me reach my lifelong dream. Unfortunately, this didn't happen. My husband's "demons" got in the way of a fulfilling relationship. I had these dreams of being married forever; but when the person I married turned out to not be the person I married, I had to re-evaluate my relationship.

My husband was an alcoholic. As I began to make plans toward my dream of getting a Master's degree, his illness pulled me away from it. I found myself in a lopsided marriage. I became the sole breadwinner and carried the emotional weight of raising a child without help and dealing with a relationship that had gone south.

Some people have asked me if I saw the signs prior to getting married. I did. But my insecurities didn't allow me to pay attention to them or

truly acknowledge their existence because I wanted so badly to marry my "Knight in Shining Armor."

Five years after my divorce, I am now focusing on me, what's important and what God has for my life. I had to make sure that, in addition to being a good mother, I still had the energy to make my dreams a reality.

Desiree's family situation wasn't ideal. It caused her to not be able to realize her dream at the time she wanted.

Sometimes we have to put our plans on hold. A step back is not necessarily a permanent setback. We often have to make adjustments on our way to our dream.

SANDY STEIN'S STORY—
SLAYING THE
GREEN-EYED MONSTER

MY husband was sure I couldn't sell my product, Finders Key Purse. He told me I couldn't make a business out of one item. I don't have any parameters of failure. It came from heaven. If heaven speaks, you better listen.

No matter how many people tried to dissuade me, I wasn't going to not do it.

One of the obstacles was the green-eyed monster. My husband hated that I was successful. He became very jealous and tried to sabotage the business. That was the biggest and most awful obstacle. I did not have the support of my spouse; he became my enemy.

I also had a bunch of copycats. Though I had a patent, a Chinese company came after me with all their might. There are a lot of bad people *who, if they see something good, they want it and will take it. I had to take them to federal court which was a long, strenuous process. It cost over $1 million to go to court. I had to either defend my business or they would take over. They later filed bankruptcy.*

As Dr. Ali mentioned, "It's lonely at the top." Unfortunately, everyone is not going to be on board with you. When it's the person closest to you, the cut seems deeper. The person closest to Sandy was trying to stop her dream.

When our spouses are not on board, it can hurt. Don't press the delete button on your dream just because your spouse doesn't see what you see.

CAPTAIN LAURA'S STORY–
FLYING SOLO

WHEN I was fifteen, I made a list of what I liked and what I wanted to do in life. I wrote a description that included my love for the outdoors, meeting different people, traveling... I thought I could be a cruise ship director, work at Club Med, be a park Ranger or even a flight attendant. I was asked, "Why don't you become a pilot?"

This was over thirty years ago, and there weren't many female pilots back then. I went to the Career Center at my school and they told me, yes, you can do this. I was so excited I ran home tell my mother. "I think I want to be a pilot." "That's crazy!" she said. "You either have to take flying lessons or go into the military. I can't afford flying lessons and you are not going in the military. It's probably just another phase that you're going through." I was completely deflated.

Things were tough at home. My mom was an alcoholic and very abusive. When I told my father, who was divorced from my mother and lived in another city, about my plans, he said, "Are you crazy? Women don't fly!"

That was the "support" I received from my family. I thought, If this is something I really want, I have to make it happen on my own without their support.

Captain Laura knew early on what she wanted to do. Her dream was to fly airplanes. Though she didn't have the support of her immediate family, her parents, she made the decision to move forward. . .without their blessings.

Are the people closest to you trying to push you away from your dream? Make the decision to not let their lack of support keep you from making your dream a reality. Remember, the dream is yours. . . not theirs. Only *you* are responsible for making it come true. Yes, it's easier with support. But if you find yourself without it, don't drop the dream.

PART 3–FINANCES

THE importance of money flows from it being a link between the present and the future.[10]

—John Maynard Keynes, Economist

A lack of finances can derail your dreams. If you want to sail the oceans, you must purchase the equipment—a boat, navigation system, food, proper clothing, and maybe a professional to help guide you along your journey. Some dreams may require a significant investment. I found that competing in a bodybuilding contest can have you digging deep into your pockets. The extra food and supplements, trainers, coaches and nutritionists, posing outfit and entry fees. . .it all adds up. If the competition isn't in your hometown, there are transportation and lodging costs as well.

If you find yourself short on cash, do the best you can with what you have and begin to think creatively about raising additional funds.

[10]John Maynard Keynes, www.azquotes.com/quote/157169

There are now crowdfunding sources, such as GoFundMe, Indiegogo, and Kickstarter that can help you raise money toward your dream. Call on friends and family to help. Don't let not having money stop you from experiencing the exhilarating feeling when you've finally accomplished your dream. Finances are nothing more than obstacles. They can be jumped over, knocked down, and circumvented. They can be overcome. If you want something badly enough, you will find a way to make it happen.

Dr. Ali says that you need to have a solid game plan when it comes to finances. "If you're building a business and you're starting something from scratch, it makes good fiscal sense to know (as much as possible) how you will survive financially during this period of achieving your goals," she said. "For instance, if you're going out on your own and you're not going to receive a steady paycheck initially, you have your strategy in place to manage your expenses. Pay down some of your debt before you pursue your dreams so that you can be free to do what you need to do. This is the best route to take, because it will allow you to focus on your dreams uninterrupted. Whether you use money you have saved up to sustain yourself, take a severance package from your job, or you have a spouse who can help you manage your expenses, you will need to have the means to fund your new opportunity as well as pay your bills."

Everyone has a relationship with money. Some of us like to save it. Others like to spend it. Many want to invest it. If you need to finance your dream, recognize what your relationship with money is like and then make the necessary adjustments. For instance, if you like to spend money, you may need to create a savings plan.

LAURA PAJESTKA'S STORY– UNDERSTAND YOUR OPTIONS

I WAS sixty-one when I started my company, MJP Trucking after working as a nurse for thirty years. The hardest part was getting financing. No one wanted to help me because my company was less than a year old, which is considered a high risk in the trucking business. I also didn't have the large revenues required for banks to approve my loan.

I read an ad that said, "We guarantee loans to small and new companies." I went to the Small Business Association (SBA) who gives banks the authority to determine whether you are credit-worthy or not. I was surprised to find out that the SBA does not have the authority to work with small and new companies.

This was very difficult to overcome. I had to pull from personal finances and alternative lenders. Alternative lenders will help you, but they have higher interest rates and stricter terms.

I was able to get a microloan to help buy office equipment. This was the help I needed. Otherwise, I would have had to max out my credit cards or borrow from family.

Some of the alternative options are great. Learn where the best sources are that will not hurt your business.

I started my business because I retired from nursing, not life. I wanted to be creative. . . to keep going. Trucking has been in my family since I was born. My father was a trucker. It was a natural fit for me.

Laura took the time to explore her best options when it came to financing her business.

Never feel as though you don't have options. You do. There is never just one alternative. Find a way to be creative when it comes to helping you finance your dream. There is plenty of money out there and many ways to get it. You have to put the time in to get the dime out.

DARRYL DOUGLAS' STORY–
DO WHAT DOESN'T COST

I ALWAYS wanted to be a clown. When I graduated high school, I investigated how to have a career as a professional clown and found a clown school in Kansas City, Kansas. The tuition was around ten thousand dollars. I didn't have it. What I did have was a scholarship to attend my local community college.

Lack of money never stopped my dream. I am a firm believer in doing what you can, where you are, with what you have. So a failed marriage setback, paying child support, saving for my daughter to attend college. . . all of this played a part in limiting what I could spend money on to pursue my dreams.

However, there is so much one can do that doesn't cost anything. If you're pursuing acting, you can perform in community and church plays. You can volunteer, do your research, and support others who have similar *goals. To use lack of money as a reason to not chase your dream s*i*s sometimes valid, but oftentimes it's a damn excuse. Do whatever you can to get ahead. Don't keep waiting until the money comes.*

After almost forty years, my deferred dream became a reality. I became a professional clown. The experience was short-lived, but it was one that I enjoyed.

Darryl was unable to immediately finance his dream of becoming a clown. However, as time passed and "life happened," he realized that continuing to move forward is the best way to reach your dream.

Is lack of money stopping you? It shouldn't. Find creative ways to continue to advance your dreams.

CAPTAIN LAURA'S STORY–
KNOCK ON THE SIDE DOORS

I WANTED to be a pilot. I didn't have the money for school, so I worked several summer jobs just to pay for flying lessons.

I decided to go to college so I could the best pilot possible. After I got my private pilot license at age seventeen, I was accepted at Embry-Riddle Aeronautical University, the "Harvard of the Skies," and was very excited. However, my mother flipped out about me going to the school. "You will not go there," she told me. "What are you doing? There is no way I'm going to let you go to that school!" she yelled at me.

I was crushed and totally destroyed.

I left home at seventeen and worked three jobs trying to pay for military school. I begged for financial aid and kept getting turned down. I couldn't understand why. I was living on my own and making very little money. It turns out my mother was claiming me on her taxes. It hampered my ability to move forward.

I was one of only a few people who were on their own in college. I was not being helped or supported by my parents, and student loans only covered so much.

You can't let circumstances hold you back from what your dreams and passions are, especially if you're trying to make the world a better place. it. If the front door doesn't work, you have to knock on the side doors, the back doors, break in a window... You can get in there. You just have to believe.

Captain Laura was faced with limited means to finance her education. Although she didn't have the support from her parents, her desire to become a pilot was far greater than her limited funds.

Think of when you were determined to have something...*anything.* What did you do to make sure you got what you wanted? Go back to that place and pull from that dogged determination that was there before.

CONGRATULATIONS!
YOU'VE JUST COMPLETED THE FIRST THREE FS IN OUR 7-PART F SYSTEM. TO RECAP:

Fear—It can prevent even the most ambitious person from taking the first step toward a dream. Fear is a paralyzer. In order to move beyond it, you have to do it. . . Take that first step, even if you're afraid. Do what you want to do even though you may have butterflies flitting around in your stomach. Find ways to help get you through the fear: Prayer/meditation, positive self-talk, encouragers, or the determination to prove the naysayers wrong. Soon your fears will disappear because the stress of *thinking* about what can go wrong is over. You are no longer thinking. . . you are *doing*.

Family—Yes, we love our families, but they can sometimes be dream destroyers. Whether the derailment is a parent, siblings, spouse, or family friend, you have to treat the dream killers as though they are strangers on the street. Understand that dream killers project *their* fears on *you*. Ignore their objections and keep moving toward your goal.

Finances—The lack of money to start your business, pay for tuition, or buy the boat in which you'll sail away into the sunset—all are very real obstacles. Consider traditional or creative ways to fund your dream. Save in advance. Try the latest in crowdfunding options or the traditional way by using savings or money market accounts. Ask for help. Other people want to see you succeed.

Now that we've covered the reasons most dreams lie dormant, we'll review four ways to keep your dreams alive, thriving, and eventually realized. Of course, there are more than the following four ways, which include: Faith, Focus, Fortitude, and Forgiveness. However, I intended to make this book accessible. It's a quick read, inspirational guide to get you moving in the direction of your dreams.

PART 4—FAITH

"FAITH is taking the first step, even when you don't see the whole staircase."[11]

—Rev. Dr. Martin Luther King Jr., Civil Rights Activist

If you start with faith as small as a tiny mustard seed and remain laser-focused with determination and fortitude, you can move mountains (see Matthew 17:20).

We know what faith is; we've all experienced it. It is believing that the sun will rise and the rain will fall. As a Christian, I learned about the importance of faith very early in life. I learned that faith is essential because there are so many unknowns. In the words of singer George Michael: "You've got to have faith."

Hebrews 11:1 (King James version) says, "Faith is the substance of things hoped for, the evidence of things not seen." Simply stated, faith is believing in something that you don't see, like the fact that once you start driving, you will eventually reach your destination.

[11]Rev. Dr. Martin Luther King Jr., www.azquotes.com/quote/158971

In Marita Mister's book *Sleeping with the Enemy: Becoming One of Satan's Lovers,* she writes, "Faith is receiving the impossible, believing the impossible that the improbable manifests."[12] The late Bishop Bill McKinney repeatedly reminded us with a similar revelation, "Faith is seeing the impossible, believing the improbable, and getting up and acting like it's possible."

Verses in Hebrews 2 through 32 continue with stories of the people who moved through life with their faith strongly tied to their futures. Hebrews Chapter 11 is so powerful that I've chosen to include it in the Appendix.

Faith without works is dead.

—James 2:26 (KJV)

It's not enough to have faith. You must put *action* toward that faith. For instance, you can have faith that you will find a job, but you have to *actively* search for employment. Your new potential employer will not text you and provide your start date if you haven't had previous contact.

While training for the fitness contest, I kept my focus on a poster of a twenty-something beauty whose body was "to die for." Did I think I was going to look like her? No...I had realistic expectations. But I thought about what my mother would always say: "Reach for the moon, and you may land upon the stars." I knew if I reached for that body, I'd end up with something in between. Maybe.

We can never move beyond where we are without faith. It is moving ahead, while not knowing the exact outcome, but believing that the

---

[12]Marita Mister, *Sleeping with the Enemy Becoming Satan's Lover* (Mustang, OK: Tate Publishing & Enterprises, LLC, 2012), 121.

outcome will be what it should. You won't know for certain that the decision you make is the right one, but you can *believe* that it is. Your *belief* will carry you through to the desired outcome.

I've heard it said that you cannot walk in fear and faith at the same time. They both cannot operate simultaneously. I believe a person can have faith that he or she will reach their destination, but also be fearful of some of the pitfalls and roadblocks along the way. What's important is that you continue to move forward, in spite of any fears you may have.

This reminds me of my favorite line said by Dory in the movie Finding Nemo: "Just keep swimming. . .swimming. . .swimming"

"We approach problems, dilemmas, and fears based on the level of courage we possess," says Dr. Ali. "Do you have the courage to perseve and move forward to achieve your dreams? The truth is, people who exercise courage *often* feel fear. However, they choose to feel that same fear and access the courage necessary to transcend their challenges. Be aware. . . The pursuit of your dreams will require you to stretch yourself to do things that require both faith in yourself and courageous action."

WENDY GLIDDEN'S STORY—
MY FAITH WAS ATTACKED
EVERY DAY

BY the time I was sixteen, I was married with two children. With a lifelong dream of becoming a famous writer, I thought that, having violated God's laws of adultery, defiance, and abortions, I was not worthy enough to have hopes and dreams.

Over time, my faith continued to increase as I sought God's hand on my life. The more we stay in His word and feed our faith, the most wonderful blessings we get to receive.

It was my faith that drew me in to seek the Lord in greater ways which in turn led me to seek a Christian life coach. It was while she was praying over me that God granted me a vision and in seeking the message behind the vision in prayer, my answer was given. That is the very moment I realized I was going to indeed become a writer.

I called upon my faith daily, but in a very major way as I was about to publish my second book. The enemy was trying to convince me that my writing was awful and that I should destroy all my written works and never write again. It was my faith in the Lord and His promises that pulled me through.

In the midst of waning confidence, Wendy realized that her faith needed to be regularly fed. It wasn't enough to have it; she had to keep it strong.

Just like the body's muscles need consistent exercise to grow strong, so does one's faith. Strong faith is a requirement to combat self-doubt and a lack of confidence in realizing your dreams.

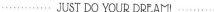

BRANDON RUSSELL'S STORY–
FAITH CANNOT BE SELF-CENTERED

I HAVE a unique experience with faith. My book is titled, Building Faith Through a Carpenter's Hands. I say "building faith" because it is truly something you must work on. Faith by definition is: Strong belief or trust in someone or something.

In my journey, my faith was centered around myself. You can have faith in yourself, but do not let that faith be self-centered and place you before God. It was not until I learned to have faith in God's image of me, and fully trusted in His vision and purpose for me, that true confidence came. It was the confidence that wiped away all fear of the unknown.

The more you live for God and glorify Him and His purpose for you, the stronger your belief and trust builds within your faith. This results in a faith so strong, you are left without doubt or fear to succeed and accomplish all the things you set your heart and mind to.

I've heard some people say that they rely on faith in what they know *they* can do. Brandon's faith in God gave him the confidence to do what fear would not allow.

Where is your faith? Search your heart. Are you relying on you, or are you relying on God?

KIMBERLY POWELL'S STORY—
FAITH IS ALL I HAVE

MY faith means everything to me. I credit my resilience to my awareness that I am inextricably connected to the all-powerful God who resides within me. I now own a socially conscious gourmet snack food company in Atlanta, Georgia.

One day I was without a job for reasons described by the industry as "downsizing," "upsizing," or "rightsizing." Many years later, I was without employment again, but knew that I could face the challenge with strength and courage, because I had developed a solid foundation rooted in faith. I am now free to pursue the expanded vision of my life which I have been predestined to fulfill. I'm more spiritually focused. I began the work to change old mindsets and erroneous beliefs about who I truly am and what is undeniably possible. I have come to realize that spiritually we are profoundly more powerful than we oftentimes choose to believe we are.

If you really believe and trust God, it's hard to give up on your dreams. My greatest fear is that I will disappoint God if I quit before I fulfill my God-ordained purpose in life. I was created to persevere and destined to win! If you truly have faith and trust in the power of God within you, it becomes virtually impossible to give up on the pursuit of your life's divine purpose. As I create my business, I understand that the journey is more about the actualization of my highest spiritual self.

When faced with uncertainty and challenges, both Wendy and Kimberly stood on the foundation of their faith to get them through the difficult times.

If you have a relationship with God, lean on Him and your faith which can be, "as small as mustard seed" to get you through the difficulties and challenges that may arise when you're moving toward your dream.

DARAH ZELEDON'S STORY– FIND A WAY

MY faith kicks in when I put forth my best effort and I'm doing everything I can do. I learned that you can't do more than that. There's a point of overkill; if you do too much, it's not beneficial. If you hold too tightly to the results you want, it will slip through your fingers.

Worry is a useless waste of emotions. It doesn't solve anything. Worry is the antithesis of faith. So is anxiety. If you have a lot of anxiety, you are not trusting the process. You want to have control. You're getting anxious because you can't control the situation. Find a way to handle it naturally by practicing yoga, exercising, and living clean.

I realize that as long as you're doing something to improve your situation, God, the Universe, will conspire to help you as long as you're working hard and moving in the right direction.

Diana Nyad, the sixty-four-year-old who swam from Cuba to Florida said, "Find a way." When I'm in a situation and I want to give up, I think of her. When your mind is blocked and you can't find a way, you have to be intuitive enough to say "stop." Reboot and assess the situation when your mind is decluttered and then move forward.

If you're going through a tough time, or if you're stressed, you should never take a mind-altering substance. You need to be clear-headed and at your best. Any time you try to anesthetize your situation, it's going to make matters worse—even if it's only one glass of wine.

Have faith that no matter what you're going through, your circumstances will eventually change. That's the nature of time. It will move you out of a situation just like it moved you into it. You have to stay the course and wait it out.

Darah understands that if you worry or are anxious about your situation, it can affect your faith.

If you have faith, there is no room for worry. Faith is knowing that your best efforts will glean desired results.

CHAPTER 5–FOCUS

FOLLOW ONE COURSE UNTIL SUCCESSFUL

YOU will never reach your destination if you stop and throw stones at every dog that barks.[13]

—Winston Churchill, Prime Minister of the United Kingdom

When I decided to compete, I was sure of one thing: I didn't know what I was doing.

I had never competed. I was a gym rat, having lifted weights for more than twenty-five years, but I didn't know the first thing about how to prepare for a competition.

[13]Winston Churchill, www.wisdomquotesandstories.com/you-will-never-reach-your-destination/

So I asked around. I was told I needed to talk to someone who had competed—someone who knew how to coach me. I needed a personal trainer, someone who would show me the exercises and the proper way to perform them. Then I also needed a nutritionist, the person who could counsel me on what to eat and when. I also needed to know how to pose, what to wear, and the ins and outs of the competition "game."

I discovered that competition is not a solo gig. I needed a team. So I assembled one. Not only did my team help me reach my goal, they also helped me to focus.

Have you ever done something and then decided, for whatever reason, that you didn't want to do it anymore? Well, I wanted to stop training. Why? Because I

...was tired

...ached all over

...wanted to sleep in

...didn't feel like working so hard

...knew I wasn't going to place in the competition anyway

...had something better to do

...was afraid.

Now, had I not had that wonderful circle around me—people like my coach Pam, who had competed for eight years—telling me to stay the course, I would have quit.

There were my personal trainers, Tony and Carl, who motivated me to continue the routine they created for me. When I wanted to get off the treadmill after ten minutes (I was told to run thirty), Carl wouldn't allow me to be a slacker.

I needed Tony and Carl. I could not have competed without them. I wasn't strong enough. They knew that eventually the body gets stronger, but sometimes the mind gets weak. When people ask me how I persevered, I tell them it was mostly mental. Yes, there was a strict diet and a workout routine that had to be followed, but if I had given up, then all the dieting and working out wouldn't have done any good.

Then there was Mike, who worked with me on my diet. I learned that in competition, what you put into your body is just as—if not more—important than the amount of time and energy spent working out at the gym.

Lastly, my cheering section is what ultimately got me through. My husband, Todd, never raised an eyebrow the times I went to the gym at midnight. I had to get my workouts in. My mother never complained when I rushed out of the house and left our young children in her care.

The best way to lose weight is to eat six small meals a day (which seems so contradictory). This meant that I had to cart my food with me wherever I went. If I was in a meeting and it wasn't lunchtime, I still had to pull out my food and eat. I occasionally got the, "Girrrl, I couldn't do that. I don't know how you do it… " Those words, and many like them, only fueled my desire to reach my goal. My nutritionist and trainer would often remind me, "If it were easy, everyone would do it."

***

My mother loved "the horses," as she called them. She enjoyed going to Thistledown and Northfield Park to watch them race. Thistledown featured thoroughbred racing and Northfield Park had harness racing. Mom also got a kick out of betting on them and sometimes winning "a couple of dollars."

The first time I saw horses at the racetrack, I asked about the "black things" they wore on their faces. "Those are called blinders," my mother explained. "They help the horses stay focused. It prevents them from looking to the side, where they can be distracted by the other horses or anything else that may slow them down."

The bottom line is this: You need to wear the proverbial blinders and stay focused until you complete your dream. There were days when I crawled out of bed and cried all the way to the basement. I got on the treadmill the entire time thinking, *Why am I doing this?. . . Why am I doing this?. . . Why. Am. I. Doing. This!?* There is one thing I did know: I wanted the outcome. To finally compete!

"Fix in your mind that you will overcome all obstacles. When you truly determine this, the dawn will start to appear."[14]

–Lincoln Patz, Owner, Success Wallpapers

Dr. Ali agrees that it takes a huge amount of focus in order to realize your dream. "Some people may not be aware of all of the distractions that can ultimately keep them from achieving their goals. One dis-

[14]Lincoln Patz, www.successwallpapers.com/wallpapers/0038-fortitude.php.

traction could be other people who may not quite understand what you are trying to accomplish and may put pressure on you to commit to other things. Another could be your own personal doubts about whether you can pull it off. There are also many other things and events that will inevitably distract you," she says.

"People who are able to realize their dream understand they must have a vision strong enough to not allow the distractions of life to take them away from it. There may be people who might not understand that your plans and motives and may distract you consciously or unconsciously. Or *you* might have doubts. . .your very own doubts can be distractions that keep you from being focused.

"Focus takes incredible discipline. But more important than discipline, you need to have a 'why.' *Why* are you focusing on this particular dream? It has to *mean* something to you. If your dream doesn't scare you, it's not big enough. If it doesn't make you wonder, *What in the heck am I doing?* It may not be big enough.

"You want to be sure that you are clear about what you're after in terms of your dreams. Then you must make decisions along the way that are in alignment with those dreams. You may miss several outings with friends and other fun events. You will have to make hard decisions to use that time to prepare for a presentation, study, practice, or write a few more chapters in your book. Those are the things that will move you forward toward your goals. You have to be focused enough to avoid the pitfalls associated with becoming distracted," says Dr. Ali.

It reminds me of an interview with multi-gold medalist, Simone Biles. She won seventeen gold medals, four in the 2016 Olympics and ten in the 2013, 2014 and 2015 World Championships. She won two gold medals in the 2015 American Cup and two in the 2016 Pacific Rim

Championships. Biles said she missed a lot of social activities in which most people participate at her age because she was focused on training and winning. She decided to fully commit to gymnastics when she was fourteen years old, leaving public school and opting to be homeschooled. She didn't attend Friday night football games, homecomings and proms—activities endeared by most youth her age.

"I never wanted to give up gymnastics," Simone said in an online article. "I did miss public school and the chance to be with my friends. That was hard, obviously. But I just couldn't give up what I had started."[15]

Dr. Ali mentions that you have to really know that there are great things on the other side—when your dream is finally realized. "That bliss you will eventually feel is something you definitely want to continue to picture in your mind so that you can maintain your focus. This might mean creating a vision board, which will help you keep your dreams front and center, so that your subconscious builds itself around your vision and your actions help make it a reality," says Dr. Ali.

I want to take you back to Sandy Stein, who was mentioned briefly in Chapter 2. Sandy made millions the first year she created and sold Finders KeyPurse. Most people would have given up if they didn't have support from their spouse. That's often not an easy path to take. But Sandy didn't give up. She was determined that she was going to create her product *no matter what!*

That's what you have to do. You must say, "No matter what, I am going to do this." Why? Because you *will* have difficulties, roadblocks, and

---

[15]Lars Anderson, "Simone Biles: From a Girl Without a Home to an Olympian on Rio's Center Stage." Bleacher Report. (August 3, 2016) www.bleacherreport.com/articles/2653490-simone-biles-from-a-girl-without-a-home-to-an-olympian-on-rios-center-stage (accessed September 1, 2016)

setbacks. I promise you will. What you need to do is remember *who* you are and *why* you have your dream in the first place. It's in you. It's your God-given purpose.

In Rick Warren's book, *The Purpose Driven Life*, he writes, "Every plant and every animal was planned by God, and every person was designed with a purpose in mind."[16]

[16]Rick Warren, The Purpose Driven Life. (Grand Rapids, MI: Zondervan, 2002), 23

JIM STEVENS' STORY–
DRAW STRENGTH TO STAY FOCUSED

I AM legally blind, having lost most of my vision while serving in the U.S. Army. I am also an award-winning artist, creating monofilament and abstract linear paintings. In order to create, I have to switch back and forth between five different lenses. Some of them I purchased; some I made for myself. Some bring things a little closer and some push things away. I constantly switch back and forth, because I can't see everything at once. This requires an extreme amount of focus.

I draw my strength from a little thing that happened in 2001. In 2000, even with my blindness, I decided I wanted to be an artist. I went through two frustrating years of destroying what I had created, punching holes in walls and throwing my art across the room. One day, my youngest,

who was twelve at the time, picked up a piece of my art, set it in front of me, and said, "Daddy, you promised not to quit." I draw strength from that everyday. Not only do I have to physically be laser-focused in order to do my art, I also have to stay focused and not let my challenges keep me from doing what I love to do.

It's amazing how lucky you are when you put in the work to get there.

Jim has a disability—he's legally blind. Yet, he decided it was not going to stop him from realizing his dream of painting. An award-winning artist, Jim's daughter gives him the laser-focused determination he needs to realize his dreams.

Is there something or someone you can access to keep you focused on your purpose?

DIANE RANDALL'S STORY—
YOU HAVE TO SET BOUNDARIES

YOU have to set priorities, and you need to decide what is most important. I had my children, who are a big part of my life. And I had to stay focused on building the business that I was trying to get off the ground at that time. So I made time a priority. There were days when I would put in two hours before leaving for work, getting up an hour or two earlier to do something for my business.

I looked at my priorities and recognized that I couldn't do it all. I had to figure out what was important to me in the moment. Did I have to give up something? Yes. I set boundaries around my time, which is always very important. If you set priorities and you don't protect them with boundaries, you are doing yourself a disservice.

If I get invited somewhere, I don't have a problem telling clients or friends or family that I only have one hour.

I will go into corporations and come out with clients. They want to go out in the evening and catch up and chitchat. I don't want to be rude; but if I have something to do in the evening, I will tell them it's not a good night.

Sometimes we feel as though we have no control. We do. You have to examine your priorities. What can you do to simplify your day? How can you find and hour in your day to do what is important?

Diane realized that it was important to set boundaries in order to stay focused on her goals. She didn't hesitate to say **no** to colleagues or family members who wanted to take up her valuable time.

Sometimes you have to set boundaries and let others know what those boundaries are. If you only have a certain time to commit, let it be known. We can't get the time back we waste while on the way to our dream.

SANDY STEIN'S STORY— TAKE IT STEP BY STEP

STAYING focused is easy when you see the light at the end of the tunnel. For me, the prize was the journey; it wasn't really the prize. I wanted to show everybody that "I could" since so many people told me I couldn't.

When doing what you need to do to achieve your dreams, there's an end, there's a beginning. . .and then you slice it into steps to reach your goal. It's easier to focus when you take a little portion and move on to the next little part and then the next little part. Otherwise, it will likely be too overwhelming. When you accomplish a small portion, celebrate the victory and then move on to the next part.

You need to be focused when you have so many projects going on like I do. When an idea comes into your head, it means you're supposed to do it. You may think that it's too hard. Or maybe you don't have the money. But down the road, somebody else might run with your idea. If

you put your idea out there and somebody else does it, you know that you can do it!

Focus comes after you begin.

It may help to recall that old riddle: *How do you eat an elephant? One bite at a time.* How do you do your dream? One step at a time.

If you're able to take the big vision you have and slice it into smaller pieces, you may be able to better focus on what you need to do to accomplish your goal. Don't look at the elephant. Look at the smaller task that's right in front of you.

PART 6–FORTITUDE

"WHETHER you come from a council estate or a country estate, your success will be determined by your own confidence and fortitude."[17]

–First Lady Michelle Obama

When I was in college, there was a fraternity on campus that often chanted, "It takes heart, determination, and fortitude."

Yes. It. Does.

Fortitude is having mental strength. It's what fuels courage. It's what the cowardly lion needed to energize his courage. Fortitude is defined as "inner strength when facing adversity or difficulty."

Think about your life and a time when you know you exhibited fortitude. If you did it then, you can do it again. You can muster up the fortitude to face your fears and begin to experience the dream you desire to fulfill, the one I believe God placed within you.

[17]Michelle Obama, www.brainyquote.com/quotes/quotes/m/michelleob415511.html.

When I broke my thigh bone in half, the doctor told me that I would probably always walk with a limp. For some reason, I didn't believe it. I absolutely could not imagine walking with a cane for the rest of my life. I was only nineteen! So I worked hard to prove the doctors wrong. There were days when I had to put a pillow over my face so I could scream at the top of my lungs while the physical therapist worked with me. I was in so much pain that I almost passed out. However, I endured each and every painful situation. I knew that if I didn't, I would never reach my goal. I sincerely believe that had I listened to the doctors, I would still be walking with a cane.

It is said that Donald Trump, business mogul and 45th President of the United States, " . . . Trusts no one and places a premium on revenge." His outlook is that he "always gets even. . ."[18]

I also believe in revenge. But it's not quite the same definition as Trump's. My revenge, or "getting even," is proving the doubters wrong. If someone doesn't believe I can do something, I get my revenge by forging ahead and doing it. It's an inner challenge to *myself.* The doubter is never involved and may never know of my accomplishment. I don't have a rub-it-in-your-face attitude; I only want to succeed so I can eliminate the external negative messages and replace them with internal, positive self-talk.

When I wanted to attend graduate school, I applied at the University of South Carolina. The then Dean of the business school sat across from me and said that I would *never* get an MBA. I sat there, stunned. *Did he just say that? Did he say it because I'm. . . Black? Female? Didn't have a 4.0 GPA? What would possess him to say that to me?* Man. That

---

[18]Scott Glover, Maeve Reston, "How Donald Trump Sees Himself," (April 1, 2016) www.cnn.com/2016/04/01/politics/how-donald-trump-sees-himself (Accessed August 18, 2016)

hurt. But not for long. Less than one year later, the University of North Carolina offered me a full scholarship, plus a stipend, to study at their Bryan School of Business.

When do you muster up the courage to prove someone wrong? Maybe it is you—your own negative self-talk—that you have to silence. If you've ever had to tell someone, "That person you are talking about is not me," and you push on in spite of any derailments—whether real or imagined—then you have the intestinal fortitude to accomplish your goal.

Fortitude. It's in there. You just have to reach down deep within yourself, pull it up, and engage it.

Dr. Ali reminds us that we all have dreams, but they are split between two types of individuals. While some individuals may flirt with the concept or idea of having a dream, others will do whatever it takes to execute their dream.

"What is it that will drive you to complete your goals or realize your dreams?" asks Dr. Ali. It could be your "*why*," which represents the ultimate reason for your dream. "Why" are you doing it? Your "why" has to be big enough to keep your eye on the prize when things get tough (because they will). When you're clear about why you're working so hard toward something, it maintains your focus and quitting is not an option. When it feels as though you can't do something, your *why* reminds you that you *must*." The bottom line," says Dr. Ali emphatically, "is your 'why' will help you move through the difficult times."

There are many famous people, even legends, whose talents we enjoy and admire, who were told they "couldn't cut the mustard" and should think seriously about a different career. Consider:

Fred Astaire—"Can't sing. Can't act. Slightly balding. Can dance a little…" This was on one of his first screen tests. He later became a Hollywood and Broadway legend.

Lucille Ball—Before her iconic show I Love Lucy, Lucille Ball was considered a failed, B-list actress. Her drama instructors urged her to pursue another profession.

Jim Carey—He was booed off the stage during his first stand-up routine at a comedy club in Toronto. Later, when he auditioned for Saturday Night Live, he didn't get the part.

Walt Disney—Disney was fired from the *Kansas City Star* in 1919. His editor said he "lacked imagination and had no good ideas."

Harrison Ford—After his first movie role, a producer told him that he should get out of show business. He worked part-time as a carpenter, which sustained him until he met George Lucas.

Lady Gaga—When she was finally signed onto a major record label, Gaga was dropped after only three months.

Bill Gates—When he dropped out of Harvard, he started a business with Paul Allen called Traf-O-Data, which flopped. Luckily, they tried their hand at business again, and Microsoft was born.

Michael Jordan—He was cut from his high school basketball team. The best basketball player that ever played the game once said, "I have failed over and over and over again in my life. And that is why I succeed."

Jay-Z—When he tried to land a record deal, no label would sign him. He then established his own, Roc-a-Fella Records.

Stephen King—Carrie, his first and most renowned book, was rejected thirty times. His wife rescued the manuscript from the trash and convinced him to re-submit it.

Ang Lee—He twice failed Taiwan's college entrance exams and was turned down from attending acting school due to his bad English. Lee has three Academy Awards; two for directing Life of Pi and Brokeback Mountain. He also won best foreign language film for Crouching Tiger, Hidden Dragon.

R. H. Macy—Macy experienced many failed retail ventures early in his career. When he was thirty-six, Macy launched R.H. Macy & Co., which grew to become one of the largest department store chains in the world.

Marilyn Monroe—When she was trying to start her career, modeling agencies told her she should instead consider becoming a secretary.

Sidney Poitier—The director for the American Negro Theatre told him to get a job as a dishwasher after an audition when Poitier messed up his lines and spoke in a heavy Caribbean accent. He perfected his craft and eventually won an Academy Award for Best Actor in the 1963 classic, Lilies of the Field.

Elvis Presley—After a performance at Nashville's Grand Ole Opry, Elvis was told by the concert hall manager that he was better off returning to Memphis and driving trucks (his former career).

J.K. Rowling—Twelve major publishers rejected the *Harry Potter* manuscript. In 1996 a small publishing house, Bloomsbury, accepted it and extended a very small advance. A year later only one thousand copies were published.

Dr. Seuss—More than twenty publishers refused to accept his first children's book. He now is a household name all over the world.

Steven Spielberg—He was rejected from the University of Southern California School of Theater, Film, and Television three times. He was eventually accepted by another school, which Spielberg dropped out of to pursue directing.

Vincent Van Gogh—While alive, Van Gogh sold only one of his paintings, and that was to a friend for a very small amount of money. He continued working, never experiencing success in his lifetime. His paintings are now worth hundreds of millions of dollars.

Orville and Wilbur Wright—They were told what they wanted to do was impossible. The skeptics were proven right every single time. Until one day at Kitty Hawk, they were proven wrong.

Had any of them listened to their detractors and naysayers, we would not have *The Cat in the Hat,* airplanes, Microsoft, nor would we have been entertained by their phenomenal talents.

PROTECT YOUR DREAM

Dr. Ali cautions that we must protect our dreams, just as we protect anything that is dear to us. "You may have doubts about your dreams that creep into your mind, but you want to guard yourself from being influenced by those doubts," she says. "We're accustomed to sharing our desires and dreams with others, but that may not always be wise. People who want to protect their dreams may feel as though they have to keep all the details about it to themselves. It may be the only way to keep yourself from others distracting you and helping to remain focused."

Know and understand your audience. Who are your genuine supporters and who are your detractors? Only share your dreams with individuals who truly support you. "When you cannot identify who is a true supporter and who may be a detractor, your confidence about your dream can suffer because of it," shares Dr. Ali. "So, you have to be able to protect your dream just like you protect your child or something else you value.

"You have to develop and maintain an adequate level of confidence to realize your dream. With confidence and perseverance, no one can take away from anything you desire.

"Covet your dreams as though they were your life," says Dr. Ali.

MATT SHAWVER'S STORY– YOU MUST KEEP GOING

W**HEN** I think about my desire to be a pilot, I wanted it badly enough that I was willing to make sacrifices.

When I decided to start flying it took over my life. There was only room for work, flying, and family. I had to stop kayaking with my friend and taking vacations every year because I had to pay for flight school. It was an adjustment.

I live in a pilot house with professional pilots from around the country. Any one of these guys would rather have their dream job at home, but we're all willing to come here, do well, and exhibit the type of professionalism that will enable us to achieve our dream.

I don't pretend that it has been easy or simple for me. It's hard work. I'm up at four in the morning every day. I have to keep going. I have days when I say, "I'm not in the mood for this." But you have to put on your big boy pants and do it anyway.

Our clients expect us to get them to their destination quickly and safely every time. Even on days when it's windy and raining and everything is not going my way, I still would do this job. The days when everything is going wrong, I still would do this job. You must be passionate about it, even if it's hard. The fact that it's hard is rewarding.

Forgive yourself on the days when you feel like giving up and just cannot face one more day. Everyone has days when they can't go on. Don't beat yourself up about it. You need rest.

I am the Pilot in Command. Whenever that motor is running, I am in charge. I must make decisions about the people sitting behind me. It's an awesome responsibility. If this was my family and somebody else was flying, what decision would I make? It's the bar you use to determine whether or not you are doing the right thing.

In the song, Eyes on the Prize, which originated during the Civil Rights Movement, the charge is to hold on.

Matt explained fortitude. It is telling friends no when they want to hang out on a Saturday night. It's getting up at four in the morning when your body is telling you it needs more rest. It's holding on no matter what until your reached your goal (the prize).

DONNA W. HILL'S STORY– A BLIND WRITER'S JOURNEY

SINCE childhood, fear has played a major role in my life, hindering my progress socially, academically, and privately. By high school, the fear was so intense that each day, upon arriving at school, I ran straight to the bathroom to be sick. Learning how to keep fear in check, to limit its destructive impact on my physical health and to proceed, often despite its presence, has been at the root of the biggest challenges of my life.

There were three basic causes for my fear—the nature of my blindness, the bullying and isolation I experienced from my peers, and the response of the authority figures in my life.

I was born legally blind from Retinitis Pigmentosa, a degenerative disease characterized by loss of peripheral vision, night blindness, and eventually loss of central vision. At the time, in the early 1950s, no one knew much about this disease, leastwise me.

I was a prime target for bullying. From singsong taunts in first grade to more brutal "tricks" in high school, my days were littered with countless expressions by my peers that I was not good enough, not normal, and not welcome in their groups. Though the overt bullying ended with my graduation from high school, my peers have found more subtle, but just as effective, ways of communicating the fact that they are not comfortable with me, that their discomfort is related to my blindness and that there is nothing I can do about it.

The authority figures in my life—parents, teachers, community leaders—reinforced these messages. I was the first legally blind child to be mainstreamed in our local school district. There was a lot of unhappiness about it; many thought my parents should have sent me to a school for the blind. Some teachers, resenting that they had been stuck with a blind child, did nothing to stop the bullying and openly laughed along with the students.

At ten years old, I considered the possibility that everyone was right. I wondered if I had some psychological malady that put a barrier between what I should be seeing and what I actually did see. It drove me to consider, not for the last time, suicide.

My parents wanted the best for me, but they trusted the experts, who believed that learning Braille and other non-visual skills should only be mentioned as a threat to help motivate me. They couldn't accept that I actually was blind, because that was as good as a death sentence.

In the face of the consistent, and often overt, messages that I should accept that I would never be able to handle college, live on my own, or get a job or a husband, my reaction was primitive, but ended up being the foundation of my successes. I simply didn't want the naysayers to be right. I thought they might be right; I was afraid they were right, but I did not want them to be right. It's a subtle difference but a crucial one. It was the only thing I had to hang my hat on for many years.

I still encounter the same prejudices, but I've long since proven them to be misinformed. I graduated from college, lived alone for twenty years—baking my own bread, gardening, and learning the non-visual skills I should have learned in childhood. I found a wonderful husband and have been married for twenty-five years. I produced three recordings of my music and published The Heart of Applebutter Hill, my educator-recommended novel. I still have more to achieve, and though I stumble from the lingering fear on occasion, I don't listen to the negativity for long.

As a blind person, Donna had fears sighted individuals will never understand. She made sure that those who discounted her abilities would never be right and was determined to prove them wrong. Where would Donne be had she succumbed to her fears?

Are there negative predictions and dream-killing words that you never want to come true? Make sure they don't.

Note: Donna and Jeaninne's stories of fear are also excellent examples of fortitude.

JEANINNE KATO'S STORY– EMBRACING THE JOURNEY ALONE

I FACED a fear in the summer of 1976 that changed the trajectory of my life. After I graduated from college, I had planned to travel throughout Europe for six weeks with a Swedish friend. I managed to last two weeks with this medical student's verbal and emotional abuse until I realized I needed to salvage the rest of my trip and continue alone. I refused to go home early with my tail between my legs, but I was petrified to be alone on a foreign continent without friends or family.

No one can predict the behavior of another human being when we are out of our comfort zones. Unfortunately, this smart, savvy man, whom I thought I knew, failed to show his prejudice against independent, outgoing American women, before I booked my trip. I could do nothing right and soon became fodder for ridicule in the form of a one-dimensional American stereotype. For example, his following description of me with other young travelers was common: "Jeaninne could never be European, she is clueless regarding world politics, doesn't speak another language, and is way too open and friendly; you know, the typical American graduate who majored in psychology." I was gripped with fear as I contemplated continuing my trip without a guide, but I *knew there was no other way.*

When I boarded a train from Venice, Italy, to Paris, France, I began to discover the real me: the me who could navigate my itinerary from country to country; the me who could rely on friendly strangers to show me the way; the me who met amazing Europeans who welcomed me into their homes. Before I traveled alone that summer halfway around the world, I questioned my inner strength and doubted my resourcefulness. After I faced the fear of being alone in foreign lands and succeeded by having amazing experiences, I came home with a definitive purpose for my life. I worked hard to meet my goals, believing I could succeed because I proved it to myself in the summer of 1976.

I found that Swedish man forty years later on Facebook. He told me that his guilt had eaten away at him all these years for how disgraceful he treated me. Now, as a physician and father of two grown women, he told me that he dreamed of finding me and telling me that I was definitely the better person all those years ago. He was too immature at that time to deal with a more open, mature woman. Admittedly, I had immense satisfaction telling him that I was a successful educator with a published book; and, I now speak another language fluently. What's that old saying? Oh yes, the best revenge is success. However, that summer taught me that the best revenge is no revenge. If you live your bliss, no one can ever steal your soul.

Jeaninne faced her fears and pressed on. She knew that being in an abusive and demeaning situation that did not allow her to flourish was too detrimental. Even though she was out of her comfort zone, she found the courage within herself to thrive.

Think about a time when you were out of your comfort zone and you had to push through your situation. What did you pull from deep within yourself to accomplish your goal? If you did it before, you can do it again.

PART 7—FORGIVE PAST FAILURES

FAILURE is inevitable. When it happens, it's important to note that it's not the end of your dreams; it's the beginning of a new chapter...the start to what's next.

Before I started my public relations business, I tried several business ideas. It was 1993 and I had, a year earlier, been downsized from a job I enjoyed. I thought of businesses I could start and remember asking George, my graphic designer friend, to design a logo for each of my businesses. "Don't you think you should settle on one of them?" he asked. "I think you're doing too much."

"Well, I like all of them," I answered. All of the businesses were unique. The one commonality was that they were each something I loved to do. I made rag dolls and sold them at work. There was a design and marketing business where I created event and informational fliers. Since I loved working out at the gym, I decided to enter the personal training world. Lastly, there was the freelance writing business.

Only two of the four businesses made the cut. However, if I'd become disenchanted with the failed doll and personal training businesses, you wouldn't be reading this right now.

Dr. Ali says that forgiveness of past failures is key to achieving your future dreams. "Forgiving yourself for failure or past decisions should not take the wind out of your sails," she says. "People will try to fulfill their dreams once, twice, or maybe three times and may come away with a sense of failure. Failure includes information that you did not have prior to starting. It's a cue that says, 'Perhaps you should go in this direction instead of that one.' It should not define you but serve as a guide to improve the way you carry out your intentions. Failure becomes a gift when you see it as feedback you will use to change your course of action.

"Armed with the context that 'failure' provides, we can forgive ourselves and reframe the experience as positive. You now have the ability to execute your dreams more effectively because you have more intelligence and insight," says Dr. Ali.

We've completed the four Fs that will help you realize your dreams: faith, focus, fortitude, and forgiveness. These four are paramount to moving beyond the roadblocks and obstacles you may face. I once heard a message by Joel Osteen, senior pastor of Lakewood Church in Houston, Texas, in which he explained that when we are soon to realize God's purpose (our dreams) in our lives, we may experience opposition. It may take us harnessing all four Fs; faith, focus, fortitude, and forgiveness to help us push through some of the challenges we may face.

LET'S REVIEW THE 4 FS AGAIN:

Faith—Faith is believing you can. If you believe you can...you *will*. Faith allows you to dig deep, plow through, and overcome any obstacles that may arise. It's *knowing*. Have you heard the saying, "I know that I know that I know?" Sometimes, with faith, you don't know *how* it will get done, you just know that it *will*.

Focus—Follow one course until you're successful. Try not to get sidetracked by other things. You need to have clear vision. Be a racehorse. Put on your blinders and keep going until you reach the finish line.

Fortitude—Fear can stop us from realizing our dreams, but fortitude and courage are what propel us. Envision the feeling of joy and accomplishment in your mind. If these are feelings you want to experience, do what you need to do to make it happen. Have the courage to press on.

Forgiveness—When you fail, know that it's an opportunity to get information. You are finding out what doesn't work so you can make the necessary adjustments. Read about the failures of very successful people (page 83). They had to forgive themselves of any possible feelings of inadequacy in order to move ahead on the road to victory.

CONCLUSION

JUST do your dream.

This is my mantra for you: *Just do your dream.*

With these few nuggets to chew on and think about, I hope you will be inspired and encouraged. If you need more inspiration from those who chose to pursue their dreams, please visit our website at just-doyourdream.com. There you will find stories of most of the people profiled in this book. There are more than sixty-five stories, and the count is growing. My goal is to see one thousand by the end of the year. That means one thousand people who are finally living their dream! It won't stop there. Each day I hope to add more profiles of encouragement.

If you find yourself unsure of what to do or where to start, I invite you to try our results coaching, also found on our website. We can help you through the process of pursuing your dream and will keep you accountable along the way.

I also invite you to join our Just Do Your Dream! Facebook Group.

Its purpose is to help everyone draw wisdom, enlightenment, and encouragement from each other. It's a sharing community where we all pull for each other.

Lastly, make it a point to finally scratch that itch, snip that thread, or finally give birth to that "baby" that you've been carrying inside you. You know—the little voice in your head that keeps nagging you? No matter how much you ignore it, it gets louder. As I mentioned earlier, realizing your dream won't be easy. But when you finally are able to exhale and make that check mark, you won't be able to contain your excitement and exhilaration.

Now I'd like to introduce you to the two bonus Fs: freedom and flourish.

Once you've finally achieved your goal, you are free! That nagging feeling is gone. The worry and stress over whether you will *ever* accomplish your life-long dream is far removed. You are now free from your fears and apprehensions and free to move forward so that you can now flourish.

My friend, Dr. Rachel Talton, is the CEO of Synergy Marketing Strategy & Research, Inc., located in Akron, Ohio. This award-winning firm helps organizations inspire, connect, and engage with customers to flourish and grow. She is also the Chief Transformation Officer of Flourish Leadership, LLC, and the Flourish Conference for Women in Leadership.

Early in 2016, Dr. Talton released the bestseller, *Flourish: Have It All without Losing Yourself.* In her book, Dr. Talton describes what it means to truly flourish:

"To flourish is to grow luxuriantly across six dimensions, which include self-care, success, spirituality, synergy, service, and legacy..." she writes.

"In plain English, when you're flourishing two things are happening: you're successfully living your purpose, and you're doing so with a sense of joy, connection and meaning."[19]

In reading Dr. Talton's book, you are led to participate in a process of flourishing using the Flourish Model of Success, or FlourishingForward. I encourage you to purchase Flourish to help you continue your successful journey.

JUST DO YOUR DREAM!

[19]Dr. Rachel Talton, *Flourish-Have it All Without Losing Yourself* (Washington, DC: Difference Press, 2016), 20.

7-PART REVIEW

FOR the sake of the importance of repetition to aid in memory, let's review the 7 Parts again:

The three Fs that can stop us from realizing our dreams:

Fear: Do it afraid.

Family: Move forward despite the naysayers.

Finances: Plan early.

The four Fs that can help propel us toward our dreams:

Faith: Hold on in the tough times.

Focus: Follow one course until successful.

Fortitude: "Just keep swimming...swimming...swimming..."

Forgiveness: Don't let your past failures stop you from realizing your dream.

BONUS DOWNLOAD:

7 Steps to Help You Move Beyond the Three Paralyzing Fs

This quick, easy read will help give you that extra push and encouragement to keep you on track.

Visit **JustDoYourDream.com** to request your free download.

PROFILES

J UST Do Your Dream! is a movement. It's people encouraging and inspiring each other to do what they've always wanted. Why? They know the joy of accomplishment—especially when they have been holding onto their dream for many years.

In the pages that follow are stories of a few admirable people who will inspire you to *Just Do Your Dream!* What follows are abridged versions of the full stories found on justdoyourdream.com, along with many others. If you have your own story to tell, please let us know at justdoyourdream.com.

> ## "You shouldn't stop having fun just because you're all grown up!"
>
> –Robert Walton, Route 66 Guys

DON'T GIVE UP ON YOUR DREAM
Peter Barber, Cheetahs!

I DREAMED of going to Africa until I was fifty-three years old.

When I was ten and growing up in Canada, I saw a *National Geographic* magazine that featured cheetahs in Kenya. From the moment I saw that picture, I fell in love with cheetahs and Kenya. I pinned that picture over my bed, and I looked at it every night.

What made you decide to finally realize your lifelong dream?

After going back and forth from Victoria to Kenya several times, I realized I was much happier in Kenya. I really enjoyed the people I met; I loved being out in the bush doing the cheetah conservation work; I loved the animals and the environment.

What were the specific obstacles that you faced?

The biggest hurdle was just leaving everything and everyone I had known since a kid and moving on to another country and lifestyle.

What helped you get through the obstacles?

Having the support of my friends here in Kenya, and that of my kids and other family members back in Victoria really helped.

Were there people who tried to discourage you?

I had some people telling me I was being irresponsible and that I shouldn't leave Victoria; but I also had many people, including my two grown children, who supported my decision.

How did you feel when you finally accomplished your lifelong dream?

Now that I'm settled into my new life and truly living my dream, I feel fulfilled. Perhaps "complete" is a better word. In fact, it doesn't so much feel like living my dream, as just living the way I was meant to.

What advice would you give to others contemplating finally living their dream?

I guess the simplest advice, which is not really simple at all, is no matter how hard it is, follow your dream.

Read more about Peter here: **justdoyourdream.com/peter-barber**

PASSION MAKES OUR
LIVES SPECIAL
Donna W. Hill, Author

E VER since sixth grade, when I realized that the musical My Fair Lady had different writers for the original play, the music, the lyrics, and the adapted version, I wanted to write a novel that had music associated with it.

What made you decide to finally realize your lifelong dream?

I had another dream—to write a novel. Our family moved to the endless mountains in Pennsylvania. It's a rural area with seventeen acres of land. It was a huge transition and gave me the opportunity to devote more time to the novel since I was no longer performing music full time.

Born with Retinitis Pigmentosa, a degenerative eye disease, I was already legally blind by three years old. My vision got worse as I got older.

What were the specific obstacles that you faced?

Being blind wasn't the most overarching obstacle. It was trying to be the independent, productive person that I knew I could be, despite what the public thought—that my blindness was a deal breaker.

What helped you get through the obstacles?

My stubbornness.

Were there people who tried to discourage you?

I wanted to find an agent, but the publishing industry was not ready for my story—the story of an independent, free-thinking blind girl.

How did you feel when you finally accomplished your lifelong dream?

It's a wonderful feeling. I remember when I got the first test copy in the mail. To hold it in my hand, actually feel and smell it, I felt like I had finally landed.

What advice would you give to others contemplating finally living their dream?

If you have a passion, know what that passion is and go for it. That's what makes our lives special.

Read more about Donna and her story here:
justdoyourdream.com/donna-hill-author

ALWAYS THINK ONE STEP AHEAD
Tim Brown, Educator, Author

I GREW up in East Cleveland, Ohio with three siblings. Although my stepfather was not the best role model, I appreciate him marrying my mother and giving us the opportunity to move from a small apartment in Cleveland to a house in the suburb of East Cleveland. I was determined that what I saw growing up, was not going to be me. I wanted to be married. My children would have a father. They would have the experience that I didn't have.

What made you decide to finally realize your lifelong dream?

After working with boys and young men, I realized that I could relate to their struggle growing from boyhood to adulthood. I understood that my story was "uncommon."

What were the specific obstacles that you faced?

I didn't know my biological father and wondered if I was equipped to write about fatherhood.

What helped you get through them?

Looking at my boys and knowing I did a great job raising them.

Were there people that tried to discourage you?

No. By the time I wrote *Uncommon*, I had worked in the community long enough that people believed in me and encouraged me. I already had experience teaching and training boys to be young men.

How did you feel when you finally accomplished your lifelong dream?

Finishing the book and telling my story of encouragement was a blessing.

What advice would you give to others that are contemplating finally living their dream?

Just get started. You must surround yourself with people who believe in you and will encourage you. Always think one step ahead. Don't short circuit the process. Once you start, the Lord will open more doors. Be Ready.

Read more of Tim's story here: **justdoyourdream.com/tim-brown**

YOUR PASSIONS ARE
WORTH PURSUING
Annette Zito, Entrepreneur

HAVING grown up with my dad being a business owner, I always thought I'd have my own business.

What made you decide to finally realize your lifelong dream?

My dad had mused about opening a luncheonette. I good-naturedly suggested the name "KitchAnnette"—a little kitchen...my name...I was very amused.

What were the specific obstacles that you faced?

The first obstacle was thinking that my ideas weren't valid—my own self-doubts.

What helped you get through the obstacles?

Besides the supportive people in my life, my drive keeps me going.

Were there people who tried to discourage you?

There were people who did not take what I was doing seriously and dismissed my efforts.

How did you feel when you finally accomplished your lifelong dream?

Working with the Westchester Italian Cultural Center for the 1st Annual Pre-Oscar celebration in February 2015, featuring my custom menu, and being so well received while signing my cookbook for attendees has been the peak so far.

What advice would you give to others contemplating finally living their dream?

Be courageous. Your ideas are valid. Your passions are worth pursuing.

Read more of Annette's story here:
justdoyourdream.com/annette-zito

NOTHING VENTURED, NOTHING GAINED
Carol Roullard, Photography Artist

I HAD dreams, but I had to be practical. I majored in computer science so I could get a good paying job. I still longed for the day I could pursue what I really wanted to do—be an artist and author.

What made you decide to finally realize your lifelong dream?

I was diagnosed with a serious illness in 1997. Life seemed short and I wanted to at least go after those things I dreamed of accomplishing.

What were the specific obstacles that you faced?

I'm not sure why I would have thought writing a book would be easy. Writing can be very difficult. Becoming an artist was "easy" because I knew nothing about getting into art shows.

What helped you get through them?

My family and friends were and still are wonderful supporters.

Were there people who tried to discourage you?

Maybe, but if so, I don't remember or maybe just didn't seem to notice.

How did you feel when you finally accomplished your lifelong dream?

My initial dream was to write a book and become an artist. I've done both. But I found I kept expanding the dreams to include more things.

What advice would you give to others contemplating finally living their dream?

First, and it's a soundbite, "Just do it." For most people, the only thing stopping you from trying to accomplish your dream is you.

Learn more about Carol's journey here:
justdoyourdream.com/carol-roullard

HAVE A DISCIPLINE OF
DAILY ACTION
Christopher Wiehl, Actor

WHEN I was in high school I wasn't sure what I wanted to do. I liked being in front of people and entertaining. I took a drama class and I loved it. I was a theater and drama major and later became an actor.

I've acted in small parts in television shows, have been a regular on ten television series and have guest starred on 30 different shows. Examples are CSI: Crime Scene Investigation, Jericho, and Private Practice.

What made you decide to finally realize your lifelong dream?

My lifelong dream is to be an actor, filmmaker and director. Working in the entertainment business and acting is my favorite. Another dream is writing my book.

What were the specific obstacles that you faced?

Getting back into acting and writing was an obstacle. I had brain surgery and nearly died. I had to learn how to walk again. I am getting back to knowing if I can do it.

People are always willing to say what you can't do and doubt what you can do. If you listen to that negative talk enough, you will believe them.

What helped you get through them?

I have a good family. My family has been very supportive.

Were there people that tried to discourage you?

In the entertainment business people discourage you all the time. Producers, directors and sometimes other actors tell you that you can't do something. I choose not to make it personal.

How did you feel when you finally accomplished your lifelong dream?

I think dreams are always changing and movable. They are dynamic. There are certain days I celebrate the victories and that feels good.

What advice would you give to others contemplating finally living their dream?

Believe in yourself. Start small. Build. If you have a dream, don't think about how you can get it done right away. It's a discipline of daily action. Every day, do something.

Read more about Chris here:
justdoyourdream.com/christopher-wiehl-actor

EXPLORE WHO YOU ARE
Beryl Pleasants, Image Consultant

I GREW up on a cattle ranch in a county with a population of six thousand. My mother was not fashionable or interested in fashion at all. I did not have any guidance in the art of fashion.

What made you decide to finally realize your lifelong dream?

A few years ago, my husband decided to transition out of his business, affording me the opportunity to pursue my own dreams. My daughter said, "Mom, this has been your passion as long as I can remember. Do something with it!"

What were the specific obstacles that you faced?

Recognition. It's hard to educate people about what I do and that it can be valuable to them. It's education.

Were there people who tried to discourage you?

No. My husband and children were very supportive.

How did you feel when you finally accomplished your lifelong dream?

It's a joy to see light bulbs go off when someone really understands why one garment will bring many compliments and others do not.

What advice would you give to others contemplating finally living their dream?

Go for it, but do some research. Know what you're doing and why you are doing it.

Read more about Beryl here:

justdoyourdream.com/beryl-pleasants-image-consultant

FOLLOW WHAT FUELS YOUR HEART
Lori Del Genis, Dress Designer

I HAD always wanted to be a dress designer.

My mother taught me to have a practical skill to support myself and my children so that I would never have to depend on anyone else.

What made you finally decide to start living your lifelong dream?

A lovely friend, who was not a typical size, was shamed and insulted by bridal salon employees. I was so angry! Nobody does that to my friend.

What were the obstacles you faced?

I had sewn for around twenty years, but I didn't think I was good enough to go pro since I had never had formal training.

What helped you get through the obstacles?

I've learned that one doesn't need formal training to create beauty. A person can go to art school for years, and if they don't have the drive inside, it's not going to make much difference.

How did you feel when you finally accomplished your lifelong dream?

It felt like I might burst from so much happiness. There is the phrase, "my cup runneth over." For me, it **exploded** over.

What advice would you give to others contemplating finally living their dream?

Do what you know you have to do. Don't let your perceived lack of training stop you. The skill will come.

Read more about Lori here:

justdoyourdream.com/lori-del-genis-dress-designer

IT MUST BE IMPORTANT TO YOU
Reecy Aresty, Adventurer

I HAVE been a student of The Shroud more than half my life.

What made you decide to finally realize your lifelong dream?

I believed from the very beginning it was the real burial cloth. I was able to afford the trip to Milan, Italy (Turin), to see it.

What were the specific obstacles that you faced?

I wasn't turned off by what anyone thought or said to me. I made my decision years ago and was determined to see the Shroud of Turin.

How did you feel when you finally accomplished your lifelong dream?

To look at the face and crucified body of Jesus was a religious and emotional experience.

What advice would you give to others contemplating finally living their dream?

If they want to do something bad enough, go for it. The opportunity may not come up again and you will be kicking yourself the rest of your life.

Read more about Reecy Aresty's story here:

http://justdoyourdream.com/reecy-aresty-shroud-of-turin

DON'T LOOK BACK WITH REGRETS
JoAnn Tilghman,
Online Store Owner

MY grandfather owned a store that imported items from Mexico. I would go hunting through the "Easter basket grass" trying to find treasures and treats.

What made you decide to finally realize your lifelong dream?

My mother-in-law has Alzheimer's. Once, when I was visiting her, she couldn't figure out what to do with her coffee mug...she couldn't find the handle. She needed one with two handles.

That was the beginning of what is now Granny Jo Products, a company with items targeted to senior citizens. We sell a lot of our products at trade shows and online.

What were the specific obstacles that you faced?

Our dilemma was figuring out where would someone buy our products? We sell items for grandparents.

What helped you get through the obstacles?

People would say, "Why would you want to start doing this when people your age are retiring and enjoying life?" This is what I've always wanted to do, and it never occurred to me that I couldn't do it.

Were there people who tried to discourage you?

My mother was the only one who said, "What are you doing?"

How did you feel when you finally accomplished your lifelong dream?

I think when anybody opens the door, either online or manually, it's exhilarating. It's validating and rewarding.

What advice would you give to others contemplating finally living their dream?

One thing I tell people is there are still twenty-four hours in a day. You don't want to look back with regrets.

Learn more about JoAnn here:
justdoyourdream.com/jo-ann-tilghman-online-store

REALLY TRY TO MAKE IT WORK
Cindy Salvo, Lawyer

B ACK when I was in high school and deciding what I wanted to do, I thought about law because it interested me. At the time, only four percent of attorneys were women.

What made you decide to finally realize your lifelong dream?

We had a problem with another pageant, and the client wanted to sue our company. It was then that I thought, "I wish I was a lawyer and I could do something about it. . . Oh yeah! Law school!"

Did you face any obstacles?

I was older than most women when I married and was concerned about having a baby.

My age was also an obstacle.

Were there people who tried to discourage you?

My mother didn't really discourage me, but she did ask, "Do you really want to do that?"

How did you feel when you finally accomplished your lifelong dream?

It was great. It was a great feeling of accomplishment.

What advice would you give to others contemplating finally living their dream?

If it's important and it keeps bothering you, definitely try to make it work.

Learn more about Cindy here:

justdoyourdream.com/cindy-d-salvo-esq

STAY IN THE BATTER'S BOX AND KEEP SWINGING
Tony Marren, Humanitarian

I ALWAYS wanted to be the head or founder of a humanitarian advocacy project. In April 2008, I created Operation Just One Can.

What made you decide to finally realize your lifelong dream?

My theory is to bring charity to a level of exponential humanitarianism. Just donate one can.

What were the specific obstacles that you faced?

The naysayers who scoff at "another charity."

What helped you get through the obstacles?

My friends encouraged me. They told me that I would see how selfish people can be.

Were there people who tried to discourage you?

If you get told no, keep going. Say, "Thank you. Have a nice day."

How did you feel when you finally accomplished your lifelong dream?

It still feels purifying. I am a stage 3 cancer survivor. I received the diagnosis in 2012. I am starting to come out of remission. I could die any time. There are no promises, but I will leave behind a legacy that will help others.

What advice would you give to others contemplating finally living their dream?

Once you start showing a record that you are not going to quit, there is no finish line.

There's more about Tony's life here:
justdoyourdream.com/tony-marren

Author's Note: Tony lost his battle with cancer only a few months before this book was published.

BE ALIGNED WITH YOUR PURPOSE
Kelly Chapman, Entrepreneur

I WAS born and raised in Shaker Heights, Ohio, attended Case Western Reserve University and received a general MBA from the J. L. Kellogg School of Management at Northwestern University.

A self-proclaimed "hustler," I have always worked three jobs since I was in high school. One of them happens to be singing. I sang in over one thousand weddings.

People love my mac'n'cheese and for years it has been my dream to open a restaurant.

What made you decide to finally realize your lifelong dream?

I was at a point in my life where I had to make some decisions about my personal values. I realized what was important to me: 1) Doing honest work about which I could feel passionate and proud, 2) Making a difference in the world for customers, employees and those who are less fortunate (i.e. hungry families and the homeless).

What were the specific obstacles that you faced?

I knew very little about running a food business. There is so much to learn! From inventory systems, to payroll systems, quality control systems, bulk recipes, and more.

What helped you get through them?

I would be remiss if I didn't mention my faith. God sent people out of nowhere. A man came into my restaurant one day, ordered, looked around, and asked a ton of questions. I learned that he is the owner of some of the largest and most successful restaurants in Los Angeles. He is now a mentor and friend.

Were there people that tried to discourage you?

Often the people who are closest to you are the ones who will discourage you. It's because they care about you and want you to be successful.

How did you feel when you accomplished your lifelong dream?

During the ribbon-cutting at our restaurant in Los Angeles, my lips started trembling and the tears just overflowed.

What advice would you give to others contemplating finally living their dream?

Learn as much as you can about the business and the industry. If your dream allows you to fulfill your passion and makes you smile every day, keep at it.

Learn more about Kelly here:
justdoyourdream.com/kelly-chapman-entrepreneur

HAVE PASSION...
I DON'T CARE WHAT IT IS
Robert Walton, Route 66 Traveler

I HAVE been to more than twenty countries, and I've seen a lot of North America but not as much as I'd like.

What made you decide to finally realize your lifelong dream?

At some point, my friend Sal and I realized we both wanted to drive Route 66.

What were the specific obstacles that you faced?

We inadvertently picked the tornado season to do the trip. When we saw vans with "Storm Chasers" on them as we drove through Texas, Missouri, and Oklahoma, we started watching the weather report a little more closely.

What helped you get through the obstacles?

Ignorance is bliss. When you want to do something for a long, long time, the "thing" becomes more important than what could possibly go wrong or happen.

Were there people who tried to discourage you?

A lot of people in our car club said, "Are you guys nuts?! You have a car that's more than forty years old. How are you going to make it from New Jersey to California and back?"

How did you feel when you finally accomplished your lifelong dream?

When we reached the Santa Monica pier in California, I don't think Lewis and Clark were any happier to see the Pacific Ocean than I was.

What advice would you give to others contemplating finally living their dream?

There are no guarantees in life. Live your dreams today.

Read more about Bob and Sal's adventures here:
justdoyourdream.com/robert-walton-route-66

HEAL YOURSELF FIRST
Dr. Tracy Thomas, Psychologist

SINCE I was a kid, people treated me like a grownup...always talking about their problems.

What made you decide to finally realize your lifelong dream?

I was on a conference call, listening to people talk and hearing myself speak. The topics were superficial; there was a lot of posing and posturing. . .the way people do in the corporate world. I thought, *I cannot do this until I'm ninety. I have to do me, so that it's not work.*

What were the challenges?

The educational journey was tricky. I had a business background, and counseling made sense. It was a very long journey.

How did you feel when you finally accomplished your lifelong dream?

It was a metaphor for life. It felt like a lifetime journey. Learning. Struggling. I was dealing with limiting beliefs and addressing them.

What advice would you give to others contemplating finally living their dream?

My advice for anyone who is thinking about making their dreams a reality is, "What are you waiting for?!"

You are here to be you and the only way to do that is to go after what you want wholeheartedly.

Follow your dreams, and the world will be happier for it.

Read more about Dr. Tracy Thomas here:
justdoyourdream.com/dr-tracy-thomas-psychologist

STEP OUT ON FAITH
Michael Boyink, Full-time Traveler

WE were your typical home-schooling suburban family living in a thousand-square-foot ranch in Western Michigan.

What made you decide to finally realize your lifelong dream?

The transition to our kids' teen years brought home the temporary nature of our family unit. If we wanted to do something cool, adventurous, fun, and special, we had to do it **now**.

What were the specific obstacles that you faced?

Choosing and buying an RV.

What helped you get through the obstacles?

Choosing to keep the house and only travel for one year.

Were there people who tried to discourage you?

Someone commented that our kids were being cloistered. They were thinking of us all being cramped together in one RV, but we knew we were going out to see the whole country.

What advice would you give to others contemplating finally living their dream?

Just do it. If you're at a point in life where you think, *I've done all the things successful people do. Is that it? Is it all downhill from here?* Take a risk and try something.

Learn more about the Boyink's full-time travel adventures here: **justdoyourdream.com/michael-boyink-fulltime-traveler**

ONLY YOU CAN MAKE IT HAPPEN
Dr. Marisa R. Silver, Actor/Model

I HAVE always craved performing. When I was a teenager, I was modeling for greeting cards and dance calendars while attending a performing arts high school.

What made you decide to finally realize your lifelong dream?

When I saw my father dealing with his illness, I thought, *How do I want to be remembered? Why not try acting again?*

What were the specific obstacles that you faced?

It can be very challenging trying to juggle multiple businesses simultaneously. I own and operate Silverspine Chiropractic and Health and In the Zone Personal Fitness.

What helped you get through the obstacles?

My father's death seemed imminent, as we were told to plan his funeral. I am happy to say that the doctors were wrong, and my father is still with us today. It was then that I knew I had to pursue my true passions in life and that performing was in my blood.

Were there people who tried to discourage you?

Many people don't understand why I enhanced my career path to include performing. I'm not changing who I am, just following an additional path.

How did you feel when you finally accomplished your lifelong dream?

When I received my membership letter to join SAG-AFTRA, a professional actors union, I knew that my hard work had been noticed.

What advice would you give to others contemplating finally living their dream?

Fear does not care how old you are and neither should you. Life can be as exciting as you want it to be, but you have to take the initiative to make it happen

Learn more about Dr. Marisa R. Silver here:
justdoyourdream.com/dr-marisa-r-silver

BE WILLING TO TAKE RISKS
Stanton Barrett–
Extreme Sports/Stunt Man/Director

I WAS born and raised in Bishop, California. When my parents separated, we moved a lot when I was growing up. I lived in several states; North Carolina, Colorado, California, and Florida. I went to six different high schools.

My Dad was a professional stunt man and I lived with him. I was interested in a lot of things; painting and drawing, skiing, motocross, exploring, shooting guns, fishing, riding bikes, sharks and whales, climbing trees and wished to fly fighter jets.

What made you decide to finally realize your lifelong dream?

I never really 'decided' on my dreams. I've always done what I loved to do and my career as a stunt man evolved from that. I've been in over 250 movies and television shows.

What were the specific obstacles that you faced?

Most people are their own obstacle. They haven't learned how to maximize their time and be efficient, to use every second of every hour to do what it takes.

How did you get through them?

I know people who don't put in the work that it takes. They think they do, but they don't really make sacrifices. You have to be willing to take risks and put in the hard work. You have to risk sleep, pull overnighters, work days and days on end.

Were there people that tried to discourage you?

A lot of people don't have support they need to do what they want. Sometimes, you must be your own support. You have to get through the criticism, know what you want and pursue it.

How did you feel when you finally accomplished your lifelong dream?

There's always more out there to do. After creating one movie you want to do the next one and a bigger one or bigger deal.

What advice would you give to others contemplating finally living their dream?

Just do it. Don't be afraid. If you are afraid you will not succeed. You have to be willing to risk everything, because that's what it takes.

Read more about Stanton here: **justdoyourdream.com/stanton-barrett-extreme-sportsstunt-mandirector**

THINK OF PERFECT MOMENTS
Nancy Shulins, Author

IWAS forty-two and no one's idea of an athlete when I bought Eli, my first horse.

He was six, and a Thoroughbred—a racehorse—who'd been brought to the barn where I'd been taking lessons.

What made you decide to finally realize your lifelong dream?

I traded one dream—that of having a child—for another—that of owning a horse—when it became obvious that despite my efforts, being a mother was not in the cards for me.

Enter Eli. My childhood dream of owning a horse had fallen by the wayside decades earlier.

What were the specific obstacles that you faced?

There was no shortage of reasons not to buy him. He was a 6-year-old hot-head, a Thoroughbred with little training and a wicked spook.

What helped you get through them?

I was lucky in that I had a very supportive husband, as well as supportive family and friends.

Were there people that tried to discourage you?

For every supportive horse-owner, there was a detractor. The barn manager, for one, made me feel as if I knew nothing. My trainer could reduce me to tears with her harsh assessments of my performance in the saddle.

How did you feel when you finally accomplished your lifelong dream?

Buying Eli was more the beginning than the culmination of achieving my dream and he became the inspiration for my book.

What advice would you give to others contemplating finally living their dream?

Just remember to think in terms of perfect moments, as opposed to perfect weeks, months, or years. Any dream worth its salt requires effort, and that effort is ongoing.

Learn more about Nancy here:

justdoyourdream.com/nancy-shulins

TOO MUCH THINKING
CAN KILL YOUR DREAMS
Eric Broser,
Fitness Magazine Cover Model

IHAD always wanted to be on the cover of a magazine.

When I was younger, I was bullied and picked on, so I started working out. I was 5 feet, 11 inches and 125 pounds. I started seeing results, slowly but surely.

What made you decide to finally realize your lifelong dream?

In 2008 someone presented the opportunity for me to be on the cover of *Ironman Magazine*. I had been writing for the magazine, and since I'd done so much and had a great following, they wondered if I would like to be on the cover.

What were the specific obstacles that you faced?

I faced many obstacles. In the beginning I didn't get a lot of support. There were more people telling me what I could not do than what I could do.

What helped you get through the obstacles?

I ignored the naysayers and gained more supporters as I began to prove myself. As I got more involved in the industry, I gravitated to the positive people and let them motivate me. I had faith in myself and believed in myself.

How did you feel when you finally accomplished your lifelong dream?

I was very proud and beside myself. I almost couldn't believe I was looking at myself on the cover of **Ironman Magazine**.

What advice would you give to others contemplating finally living their dream?

Stop thinking about it and go for it.

Learn more about Eric Broser here:
justdoyourdream.com/eric-broser-fitness-magazine-cover

YOU MUST DECIDE 150 PERCENT
Sandy Stein, Entrepreneur

IN 1971 when I was in college, I received a post card from Western Airlines. They hired me as a stewardess.

What made you decide to finally realize your lifelong dream?

My dad came to me in a dream. He had been gone for fifteen years. He gave me the idea for a hook on one end and a lobster claw on the other. It helps you find your keys in your purse quickly. I tried it, then decided to invent and sell it.

What were the specific obstacles that you faced?

My husband was sure I couldn't sell it. He told me I couldn't make a business out of one item.

What helped you get through the obstacles?

I always wondered how I got through the tough times. I have many confidants, friends I've had more than forty-five years.

Were there people who tried to discourage you?

Definitely my husband. He was my husband and father of my son, and he was doing unconscionable things.

How did you feel when you finally accomplished your lifelong dream?

When I saw Finders KeyPurse in stores, it was like the birth of my second child. It made me feel like I actually did the impossible. I turned an idea into reality.

What advice would you give to others contemplating finally living their dream?

When you decide to live your dream, you have to give it150 percent, no matter how many people try to dissuade you.

Read more about Sandy's story here:
justdoyourdream.com/sandy-stein

IF YOU DON'T LIVE YOUR DREAM, YOU'VE ONLY LIVED HALF A LIFE
Jeaninne Escallier Kato,
Speak a New Language

I GREW up in LaHabra, California, a Hispanic neighborhood, but never truly learned to speak Spanish. It was my dream to learn the language and to love the Mexican culture.

What made you decide to finally realize your lifelong dream?

In the schools where I taught, Spanish was the students' primary language. So I made the decision to learn Spanish. In 1999, at age forty-five, I entered a community college to learn the language.

What were the obstacles you faced?

My energy and momentum was on fire. I didn't have obstacles. No one told me I couldn't meet my goals.

How did you feel when you finally accomplished your lifelong dream?

It was surreal. I am now Mexican.

What advice would you give to others contemplating finally living their dream?

If you don't live your dream, you've only lived half a life. If you don't at least try or take steps to live your bliss, you are not living a full life.

We all have negative thoughts in our lives that make us doubtful. Ignore the thoughts. Go for it.

Read more about Jeaninne here:

justdoyourdream.com/jeaninne-escallier-kato

DISABILITIES DON'T
DETER DREAMS
Jim Stevens, Artist

IN 1970, while a sergeant in the Army, I was shot in the head during a combat mission in Vietnam. Twenty-three years later, in 1993, the fragments caused a stroke in my visual cortex, leaving me suddenly and legally blind, with only a pin dot of vision remaining in both eyes.

What made you finally decide to live your lifelong dream?

I lost my job teaching at the University of Colorado, my wife left the family, and I was suddenly the blind single parent of two young daughters. In 2000, I determined to reinvent myself and become a full-time artist despite my disability and my father's earlier admonishments.

What were the obstacles you faced?

Remembering that my father told me that no son of his was going to grow up starving in an attic and struggling to relearn my craft.

What helped you get through the obstacles?

Despite the setbacks and frustrations, I refused to quit. Whenever I felt overwhelmed by the challenges in front of me, my youngest daughter would softly remind me, "Daddy, you promised not to quit."

How did you feel when you finally accomplished your lifelong dream?

Given the setbacks and obstacles I faced, it's an indescribable feeling.

What advice would you give to others contemplating finally living their dream?

It's amazing how lucky you can get when you put in the work to get there.

Learn more about Jim here: **justdoyourdream.com/jim-stevens**

KNOW ALL THE PROS & CONS
Laura Pajestka, Entrepreneur

I **WAS** born into the trucking industry because my Dad was a union driver for many years. Before my father passed away, our son had followed in his grandfather's footsteps. I wanted the business to leave as a legacy for my son, in memory of my Dad.

What made you decide to finally realize your lifelong dream?

I retired from nursing after almost 30 years. I always wanted to pursue this passion of starting my own company with my family.

What were the specific obstacles that you faced?

As a new company, everyone would think it was the fact that I'm a woman. In the banking world, the trucking industry is considered high risk for loans. The banks would not help me. My first year was very difficult.

What helped you get through them?

I did a lot of networking. I made arrangements and negotiated by working directly with unions and my clients. It helped me get over the hump.

Were there people that tried to discourage you?

No. Our family and friends, the unions and the construction industry were very supportive.

How did you feel when you finally accomplished your lifelong dream?

It was great. It's very rewarding and exciting.

What advice would you give to others that are contemplating finally living their dream?

Do your homework. Make sure that you know all the pros and cons of what you're going to deal with in your industry. Talk to the people in your industry so you will know the possible hurdles. Get advice on what you need to do to overcome those hurdles.

Have a wonderful support system. Reach out for people to help you.

Read more about Laura here:
justdoyourdream.com/laura-pajestka-entrepreneur

SUCCESS DOES NOT
HAPPEN OVERNIGHT
Cliff Simon, Actor, Author

I GREW up in Johannesburg, South Africa. In 1977, when I was 15, my parents emigrated to London to get away from South Africa's Apartheid situation.

I was a swimmer with a dream to swim in the Olympics. I trained for over six hours a day with an ex-Olympic coach.

After attending the military when I decided to not swim anymore, I didn't know what I wanted to do. I was also a gymnast. An opportunity arose for me to be on stage at the Moulin Rouge in Paris.

After an incredible year at the Moulin Rouge, I went back to South Africa and pursued modeling. I entered a competition where the prize was a Soap Opera audition. I stayed on Egoli Place of Gold for seven years.

My new dream was to be a USA citizen. I applied for my citizenship after the Soap Opera and put a timeline on my dream and turned it into a goal. I got an agent, auditioned for many Soap Operas and TV series, and landed my first job on Nash Bridges. At the age of 40, I reached my dream and goal.

What made you decide to finally realize your lifelong dream?

My dream was to come to the United States and I did it. Another dream was to write a book. In July, 2016 my book, *Paris Nights My Year at the Moulin Rouge* was published.

What were the specific obstacles that you faced?

As an actor in Los Angeles, every day is an obstacle. You hear a ton of no's and need to stay strong , single-minded and believe in yourself.

What helped you get through them?

It's making a commitment and having nothing to fall back on. My experience in the military helped me to see that.

Were there people that tried to discourage you?

No. None of my friends in South Africa told me I would never make it. When I decide to do something, I give it one hundred percent.

How did you feel when you accomplished your lifelong dream?

As it stands, my book, *Paris Nights, My Year at the Moulin Rouge* is more satisfying than anything I've ever done.

What advice would you give to others contemplating finally living their dream?

Never give up. Conformity is the jailer of freedom and the enemy of growth. Do not conform to what you think others want or need you to be. Be yourself.

Read more about Cliff here: **justdoyourdream.com/cliff-simon-actor**

EXPECT IT TO HAPPEN
Chris Rither, Korea!

W**HEN** I was about twenty-four, I made a list of forty things I wanted to do before I died. A few years later I got a computer with Windows 3.1 and made a rough poster. Over the years, I checked off my goals one at a time.

What made you decide to finally realize your lifelong dream?

By the time I returned home to Hawaii, I realized that I could no longer physically do the job I was doing, but I could stand up and teach.

What were the specific obstacles you faced?

Well, I didn't have a master's degree or a Ph.D. The US is still the most widely accepted country for higher education. Everybody wants an American diploma.

What helped you get through the obstacles?

Goal-setting, plus having a support network is great. . . and a supportive wife.

Were there people who tried to discourage you?

I ran businesses in Hawaii before moving to Korea, and most of the people in Hawaii thought I was crazy.

How did you feel when you finally accomplished your lifelong dream?

It motivated me for my next goal. I was relieved and encouraged that I could set my next goal and reach it by the time I'm sixty.

What advice would you give to others contemplating finally living their dream?

Expect it to happen. Have faith, but be realistic about it. You have to be driven, but realize it may take time.

Read more about Chris and his journey here:
justdoyourdream.com/chris-rither-korea

THINK ABOUT HOW YOU WILL DO IT
Matt Shawver, Helicopter Pilot

WHEN my parents told me I was going to have a little brother, I was sitting on the floor playing with a lunar module toy. I remember wanting to get it to work more than I wanted to have a little brother.

What made you decide to finally realize your lifelong dream?

I can remember watching Snoopy getting shot down by the Red Baron. I always wanted to fly. . . always attended air shows.

What were the specific obstacles that you faced?

Flight training is very expensive, around $55,000. It's about the same as getting a master's degree.

What helped you get through the obstacles?

It's like building the IKEA chair. How do you build it? Don't spend too much time worrying about the obstacle in the way. Figure out how you're going to go around it, over it, or through it.

Were there people who tried to discourage you? Who were they and what did they say to you?

Eighty percent of the people I knew thought I was crazy. I was paid well, had excellent benefits, and worked for America's oldest bank.

How did you feel when you finally accomplished your lifelong dream?

It felt empowering, as though I could do anything.

What advice would you give to others contemplating finally living their dream?

Do it.

Stop thinking about why you can't; think about *how* you're going to do it. Just because you can't figure it out today doesn't mean you never will.

Read Matt's story here: justdoyourdream.com/matt-shawver

SURROUND YOURSELF WITH POSITIVE PEOPLE
Nancy Redd, Musician

I HAVE been a social worker for more than twenty years but knew at the age of three that I wanted to be a musician. My family has always encouraged my music, but told me I couldn't major in it at college because I needed to have stability and a "career."

What made you finally realize your dream?

Music has always been part of my life. I put my dreams on hold. I still performed once in a while, but my focus was on raising my son.

Eventually, my son's permission helped me to pursue my dream again.

What were the specific obstacles that you faced?

Starting over as a musician was a challenge because I needed to hone up on my skills. Performing is a work in progress, and I had over a ten-year hiatus!

What helped you get through the obstacles?

I was supported by my parents and my son. My dad is also a musician. He encouraged me to be a leader.

Were there people who tried to discourage you? Who were they and what did they say to you?

Venues have hired other acts without giving me a chance. They never even accepted my information to know if I was a good fit for their venue.

How did you feel when you finally accomplished your lifelong dream?

Performing has, and continues to be, a wonderful experience.

What advice would you give to others contemplating finally living their dreams?

I tell anyone that it is never too late to pursue your dreams. Don't let anyone dissuade you.

Read more about Nancy here:
justdoyourdream.com/nancy-redd-musician

USE FAILURE AS A
TOOL FOR CORRECTION
Jim Kellner, Hypnotist

I DON'T even remember when I first wanted to become a hypnotist, but I know it goes back to at least my early teens.

What made you decide to finally realize your lifelong dream?

When I actually decided to exercise, lose weight, and eat better, I realized hypnosis actually does work in helping people lose weight. I got the confidence to do it since it worked on me.

What were the specific obstacles that you faced?

My own limiting beliefs were my biggest challenge.

What helped you get through the obstacles?

I hypnotize myself. Even before I started using hypnotism, I can remember my first monologue on stage. I felt as though I was going to die in front of the class. The need to express myself is the only way I can be happy. It's a big desire.

Were there people who tried to discourage you?

There were a few people who would say, "Wouldn't it better to have a regular job?"

How did you feel when you finally accomplished your lifelong dream?

Thank God I finally did it! What can I do next? I want to be like Tony Robbins and inspire people.

What advice would you give to others contemplating finally living their dream?

Failure is only temporary. Use it as a tool for correction.

Read more about Jim here: **justdoyourdream.com/jim-kellner**

TRUST THE PROCESS
Mari McCarthy, Singer

I WAS diagnosed with Multiple Sclerosis (MS) and had to make a clear change. At the time of my diagnosis, I had a business management consulting firm. I was living out of a suitcase, traveling to Fortune 1000 companies.

What made you decide to finally realize your lifelong dream?

I set the goal to keep ongoing goals. I read an article in the newspaper about a music school that had students of all ages. In 2000, I started taking lessons. There was something about being on stage. I can't tell you how fantastic that was. I will do anything to get on stage.

What were the specific obstacles that you faced?

I realized through the singing lessons that I was still thinking and feeling like a scared little girl. *Can I hit the high notes?*

What helped you get through the obstacles?

Journaling. . .journaling. . .journaling. I fill up tons of notebooks.

Were there people who tried to discourage you?

No. It's one of my things. . .I never listen to anybody else.

How did you feel when you finally accomplished your lifelong dream?

Oh my goodness! I got a hint of what heaven must be like.

What advice would you give to others contemplating finally living their dream?

Get out a journal and write. It will help you reach your dreams faster.

Learn more about Mari and how she triumphed here: justdoyourdream.com/mari-l-mccarthy

DON'T FORGET TO LEAP
Jeff Cannon, Coach/Guide

IN 2009 I had thirty days to fire my employees, let go of my clients, and shut down my business to get ready for an eleven-hour surgery. It ended one life, the life everyone else wanted me to live, and opened a door to a new one.

What made you decide to finally realize your lifelong dream?

It was time to take another path and pursue the dream I once had. I was ready to open up a school and teach meditation.

What were the specific obstacles that you faced?

The meditation community pushed back on the idea of creating a different type of meditation.

What helped you get through the obstacles?

People. Keep only positive people around you. I tell people to get rid of all the people who don't support you.

Were there people who tried to discourage you?

I had tremendous support from my family, which came from the idea that, "Jeff has had seven brain tumor surgeries. He deserves to be happy."

How did you feel when you finally accomplished your lifelong dream?

It feels fabulous. It feels positive.

What advice would you give to others contemplating finally living their dream?

Don't wait for a brain tumor to start pursuing your dream. Take your time; plan ahead. Line up the things you need to actually take the leap. . .and then don't forget to leap.

Learn more about Jeff here:
justdoyourdream.com/jeff-cannon-coachguide

PERSISTENCE IS PARAMOUNT
TO SUCCESS
Karen Koenig, Author

I'M in my late sixties and published my first book when I was fifty-eight.

In grade school, I loved to write poems and at camp and college penned long letters to friends.

What made you decide to finally realize your lifelong dream?

I quit my full-time job in the mid-1990s as a clinical supervisor in a methadone clinic to open a private therapy practice in Boston and have more time to write.

What were the specific obstacles that you faced?

The major obstacle was being an unknown writer with no track record.

What helped you get through them?

My agent was very supportive and had great faith in my message and my "writing voice."

Were there people that tried to discourage you?

I don't recall anyone trying to discourage me. My husband was 100 percent behind my efforts and continues to be my best cheerleader.

How did you feel when you finally accomplished your lifelong dream?

After I received a verbal acceptance of my first book, *The Rules of "Normal" Eating,* I was driving to a meeting and closed the windows and whooped and hollered with joy the whole way there.

What advice would you give to others contemplating finally living their dream?

I suggest not to listen to anyone who wants to discourage you. It doesn't get better than doing what you love. I feel fortunate to have lived out a childhood dream.

Learn more about Karen here:
justdoyourdream.com/karen-r-koenig

PERSEVERE AND KEEP
A GOOD ATTITUDE
Craig Wolfe, CelebriDucks

WHEN I graduated college with English and religion degrees, I didn't know what I wanted to do with my life. Money alone does not motivate me; passion and creativity do. Anyone can make money. It was scary not having direction for my life.

What made you decide to finally live your dream?

Well, as for the ducks, who doesn't love a rubber duck? I just wanted to do something totally creative and out of the box.

What were the specific obstacles that you faced?

The animation business: Most traditional animation art is painted by hand, but everything now is created on a computer. The hand-painted cells are on acetate. It took a long time to figure out how to print on acetate from a computer.

Were there people who tried to discourage you?

There was no one telling me no. I got input from everyone I knew, and they had many good ideas. The main question I was asked was: "Can you do it? It's not a bad idea, but can **you** do it?"

How did you feel when you finally accomplished your lifelong dream?

It was so cool.

What advice would you give to others contemplating finally living their dream?

Do it.

Know that money and fame will never satisfy. What lasts is love, compassion, and doing good.

Learn more about Craig Wolf and his companies here:
justdoyourdream.com/craig-wolf-celebriducks

YOU MUST FIND THE TIME
Philip Mandel, Concert Pianist

I'M in my sixties and now living my dream.

I retired eight years ago from a career as an engineer, which I began when I graduated college. My other career was a health coach.

What made you decide to finally realize your lifelong dream?

Music is in my bones. I love it. The only reason I didn't study music in college is my father wouldn't let me.

What were the specific obstacles that you faced?

Finding practice time was a big obstacle. I fill my life with so many fun things. I spend time with my friends, go to the gym every day. . .finding the time to practice takes discipline. I have to force myself to stop watching TV and make time to play.

What helped you get through the obstacles?

If you're going to do something, you must find the time and make it happen.

Were there people who tried to discourage you?

No. They said to me, "It's about time. What took you so long?"

How did you feel when you finally accomplished your lifelong dream?

I'm in heaven. If my parents could see me now. I like to think they are in heaven and are proud of me.

What advice would you give to others contemplating finally living their dream?

I would say: 1) Decide what you want to do. 2) Think about what accomplishing your dream will do for you. 3) If that's enough of a draw and speaks to you loud and clear, like a bell. . .go for it!

Read more on Philip Mandel, pianist, here:
justdoyourdream.com/philip-mandel-concert-pianist

NOTHING CHANGES IF NOTHING CHANGES
Shelley Rafilson, Singer/Author

I ALWAYS wanted to be thin and to be a successful singer.

What made you decide to finally realize your lifelong dream?

Due to health problems and being middle-aged and on medications that can cause weight gain, it was even more difficult to pursue my dream; but I was able to successfully use my positive mindset to lose the weight on my own, and it gave me the confidence I needed.

What were the specific obstacles that you faced?

When I was comfortable with my weight, finances were my other obstacle.

What helped you get through the obstacles?

Faith. I had a lot of health problems, and I was helping take care of my elderly father who wasn't well himself. I wanted us both to live and be happy and have a normal life.

Were there people who tried to discourage you?

People generally don't want to discourage you; however, some people want to hold you back because they are not happy with themselves.

How did you feel when you finally accomplished your lifelong dream?

I felt great and had renewed confidence to continue to pursue my life-long dream of singing.

What advice would you give to others contemplating finally living their dream?

If your dream is important to you, you owe it to yourself to try. Don't look for excuses. There is success in trying; at least you'll know you tried.

Read more about Shelley's journey here:
justdoyourdream.com/shelley-rafilson-lost-100-pounds

DREAM SO BIG ONLY
GOD CAN DO IT
Brandon Russell, Model/Actor

IT was during my freshman year at Appalachian State University that a small seed was planted by a professor teaching Introduction to Theatre and Dance. He saw something in me I did not allow myself to believe.

For seven years, I traveled all over the United States and overseas modeling for the leading fashion brands doing runway, editorial, and commercial shoots. I enjoyed it but something was still missing.

What made you decide to finally realize your lifelong dream?

I believe it was the decision to completely surrender and relinquish all worry and doubt and leave it all in the hands of God. It wasn't until then that I was chosen for Trading Spaces.

What were the specific obstacles that you faced?

Sometimes your greatest obstacle is staring back at you in the mirror. I was my greatest obstacle for so long. Location was also a factor.

What helped you get through them?

Today it is much easier than in the past due to the advancement in technology. It allows for more personal interviews across states, countries, even continents with the use of programs like Skype.

Were there people that tried to discourage you?

I had people encouraging me all the time. I believe it was my own inner self that was questioning my decisions to model and act.

How did you feel when you finally accomplished your lifelong dream?

I will do my best to describe it. It is a feeling hard to put into words. It was euphoric.

What advice would you give to others contemplating finally living their dream?

I live my life by this. . . Dream so big that only God can do it. If you can do it yourself, you're not dreaming big enough.

Learn more about Brandon here:
justdoyourdream.com/brandon-russell-modelactor

YOU MUST HAVE THE DESIRE
Iris Hirsch, Singer

E VER since I was a little girl, around five years old, I have loved music and singing. I wanted to be a singer and an actress.

What made you decide to finally realize your lifelong dream?

I found an ad on Craigslist. They were looking for a male vocalist. I reached out to them and asked if they wanted to try a female vocalist instead.

What were the specific obstacles that you faced?

When the band first started out, I was still working as a full-time teacher and data coach. It was difficult doing both.

What helped you get through the obstacles?

I keep doing research. Whenever I go out, I'll grab a newspaper and always look for venues, events, and places that are looking for entertainment. I find out whether they are interested in our kind of music.

Were there people who tried to discourage you?

People keep saying that I'm retired; and they look at my schedule and say I'm too busy for a retired person.

How did you feel when you finally accomplished your lifelong dream?

It was the best feeling. I've always wanted to be on the main stage in front of a big audience. Now I'm doing it.

What advice would you give to others contemplating finally living their dream?

Keep pursing your dream. Don't ever give up. It's never too late.

Read more about Iris Hirsch's journey here:
justdoyourdream.com/iris-hirsch

ACT ON YOUR DEEPEST DESIRE
Faith McKinney, Personal Brander

MY dream was to overcome my shyness, become famous, and meet and be seen with celebrities.

What made you decide to finally realize your lifelong dream?

I decided to act and sing to build up my confidence. I wanted to find some things I could do well. When I put my desires out there, it came to me.

What were the specific obstacles that you faced?

I'm my biggest obstacle. I'm overweight, and not tall and blonde.

What helped you get through the obstacles?

I kept moving.

How did you feel when you finally accomplished your lifelong dream?

It felt surreal. If you take control and act like you're in control, people will follow you.

What advice would you give to others contemplating finally living their dream?

Find that inner child wish and act on it. The world opens up when you act on your deepest desires. Everything aligns perfectly.

You must have a plan for your dream. Ask people who know how to live their dream.

Learn more about Faith here:

justdoyourdream.com/faith-mckinney

FOLLOW YOUR PASSION
Carol Gee, Author

GROWING up, while I imagined someday writing the great American novel, my mother and the women in my village saw me, chalk in hand poised over a blackboard.

As a teenager, I wrote poems. Later, as a single woman, poems were written to vent my frustrations with dating. Two pieces, Ode to That Lying Scum, and Swinging from Chandeliers: Does the Warranty Cover This? came about before finally finding my 'Mr. Right.'

What made you decide to finally realize your lifelong dream?

It took a big birthday staring me in the face (the big 5-0), along with that chin hair that continued to reappear, even after tweezing with industrial strength tweezers. That same one, when it returned, showed up with an entourage and took up residence around my mouth. That catapulted me into realizing my dream.

Did you face any obstacles?

No. I guess my first book wrote itself and published itself. I had a few rejections.

Were there people that tried to discourage you?

I am not easily discouraged and I didn't let the naysayers get to me. I am the biggest supporter of my books.

How did you feel when you finally accomplished your lifelong dream?

It was unbelievable. I am good at marketing and took advantage of the Christmas gift-giving season.

What advice would you give to others that are contemplating finally living their dream?

Just do it. Find ways to do it. People say I'm a role model because I am doing what I love.

Through the years, I've learned living your dream and following your passion or purpose, is not for the faint of heart.

Read more about Carol Gee here:
justdoyourdream.com/carol-gee-author

APPENDIX—FAITH

I'VE included Hebrews 11 because it shows examples of the faith of people during Biblical times. People in the Bible are just that... people. They were fearful, apprehensive, unsure, unclear, and ignorant. However, Hebrews tells the stories of many who were unmoved by fear and uncertainty, and instead were guided by faith.

[1] Now faith is the substance of things hoped for, the evidence of things not seen.

[2] For by it the elders obtained a good report.

[3] Through faith we understand that the worlds were framed by the word of God, so that things which are seen were not made of things which do appear.

[4] By faith Abel offered unto God a more excellent sacrifice than Cain, by which he obtained witness that he was righteous, God testifying of his gifts: and by it he being dead yet speaketh.

[5] By faith Enoch was translated that he should not see death; and was not found, because God had translated him: for before his translation he had this testimony, that he pleased God.

[6] But without faith it is impossible to please him: for he that cometh to God must believe that he is, and that he is a rewarder of them that diligently seek him.

[7] By faith Noah, being warned of God of things not seen as yet, moved with fear, prepared an ark to the saving of his house; by the which he condemned the world, and became heir of the righteousness which is by faith.

[8] By faith Abraham, when he was called to go out into a place which he should after receive for an inheritance, obeyed; and he went out, not knowing whither he went.

[9] By faith he sojourned in the land of promise, as in a strange country, dwelling in tabernacles with Isaac and Jacob, the heirs with him of the same promise:

[10] For he looked for a city which hath foundations, whose builder and maker is God.

[11] Through faith also Sara herself received strength to conceive seed, and was delivered of a child when she was past age, because she judged him faithful who had promised.

[12] Therefore sprang there even of one, and him as good as dead, so many as the stars of the sky in multitude, and as the sand which is by the sea shore innumerable.

[13] These all died in faith, not having received the promises, but having seen them afar off, and were persuaded of them, and embraced them,

and confessed that they were strangers and pilgrims on the earth.

¹⁴ For they that say such things declare plainly that they seek a country.

¹⁵ And truly, if they had been mindful of that country from whence they came out, they might have had opportunity to have returned.

¹⁶ But now they desire a better country, that is, an heavenly: wherefore God is not ashamed to be called their God: for he hath prepared for them a city.

¹⁷ By faith Abraham, when he was tried, offered up Isaac: and he that had received the promises offered up his only begotten son,

¹⁸ Of whom it was said, That in Isaac shall thy seed be called:

¹⁹ Accounting that God was able to raise him up, even from the dead; from whence also he received him in a figure.

²⁰ By faith Isaac blessed Jacob and Esau concerning things to come.

²¹ By faith Jacob, when he was a dying, blessed both the sons of Joseph; and worshipped, leaning upon the top of his staff.

²² By faith Joseph, when he died, made mention of the departing of the children of Israel; and gave commandment concerning his bones.

²³ By faith Moses, when he was born, was hid three months of his parents, because they saw he was a proper child; and they were not afraid of the king's commandment.

²⁴ By faith Moses, when he was come to years, refused to be called the son of Pharaoh's daughter;

²⁵ Choosing rather to suffer affliction with the people of God, than to enjoy the pleasures of sin for a season;

²⁶ Esteeming the reproach of Christ greater riches than the treasures in Egypt: for he had respect unto the recompence of the reward.

²⁷ By faith he forsook Egypt, not fearing the wrath of the king: for he endured, as seeing him who is invisible.

²⁸ Through faith he kept the Passover, and the sprinkling of blood, lest he that destroyed the firstborn should touch them.

²⁹ By faith they passed through the Red sea as by dry land: which the Egyptians assaying to do were drowned.

³⁰ By faith the walls of Jericho fell down, after they were compassed about seven days.

³¹ By faith the harlot Rahab perished not with them that believed not, when she had received the spies with peace.

³² And what shall I more say? for the time would fail me to tell of Gedeon, and of Barak, and of Samson, and of Jephthae; of David also, and Samuel, and of the prophets:

³³ Who through faith subdued kingdoms, wrought righteousness, obtained promises, stopped the mouths of lions.

³⁴ Quenched the violence of fire, escaped the edge of the sword, out of weakness were made strong, waxed valiant in fight, turned to flight the armies of the aliens.

³⁵ Women received their dead raised to life again: and others were tortured, not accepting deliverance; that they might obtain a better resurrection:

³⁶ And others had trial of cruel mockings and scourgings, yea, moreover of bonds and imprisonment:

[37] They were stoned, they were sawn asunder, were tempted, were slain with the sword: they wandered about in sheepskins and goatskins; being destitute, afflicted, tormented;

[38] (Of whom the world was not worthy:) they wandered in deserts, and in mountains, and in dens and caves of the earth.

[39] And these all, having obtained a good report through faith, received not the promise:

[40] God having provided some better thing for us, that they without us should not be made perfect.

HELPFUL RESOURCES

A S you travel along your journey to finally doing what you always wanted, know that you never have to take even one step alone. Following are a few resources (there are many more), that will help guide your steps.

BOOKS

A Woman's Worth, Marianne Williamson, Ballantine Books, 2013. With *A Woman's Worth*, Marianne Williamson turns her charismatic voice--and the same empowering, spiritually enlightening wisdom that energized her landmark work, *A Return to Love*—to exploring the crucial role of women in the world today. (Amazon)

The Path Redefined, Lauren Mallian Bias, BenBella Books, 2014. Success is not about climbing over colleagues or climbing the corporate ladder; it's about the ability to rise to your full potential and tackle challenges with enthusiasm. In today's career climate, you have to be innovative and ambitious and capitalize on your individual talents. (Amazon)

Necessary Dreams, Anna Fels, Anchor, 2013.
In this groundbreaking book about how women perceive, are prepared for, and cope with ambition and achievement, psychiatrist Anna Fels examines ambition at the deepest psychological level. Cutting to the core of what ambition can provide—the essential elements of a fulfilling life—Fels describes why, for women but not for men, ambition still remains fraught with often painful conflict. (Amazon)

Emotional Intelligence, Dan Goleman, Bantam, 2012.
Everyone knows that high IQ is no guarantee of success, happiness, or virtue, but until *Emotional Intelligence,* we could only guess why. Daniel Goleman's brilliant report from the frontiers of psychology and neuroscience offers startling new insight into our "two minds"—the rational and the emotional—and how they together shape our destiny. (Amazon)

The Four Agreements: A Practical Guide to Personal Freedom,
Don Miguel Ruiz, Amber-Allen, 2011.
In The Four Agreements, don Miguel Ruiz reveals the source of self-limiting beliefs that rob us of joy and create needless suffering. Based on ancient Toltec wisdom, *The Four Agreements* offer a powerful code of conduct that can rapidly transform our lives to a new experience of freedom, true happiness, and love. (Amazon)

What Makes the Great Great: Strategies for Extraordinary Achievement, Dr. Dennis Kimbro, Main Street Books, 2011.

According to Dr. Kimbro, being great depends on a commitment to making dreams come true: "All high achievers make choices, not excuses." He believes we all have the seeds of greatness in us, and his book gives readers the tools to discover and nurture those seeds, showing them how to motivate themselves to master every aspect of their lives. (Amazon)

Outliers: The Story of Success, Malcolm Gladwell, Little, Brown and Company, 2008.

There is a story that is usually told about extremely successful people, a story that focuses on intelligence and ambition. Gladwell argues that the true story of success is very different, and that if we want to understand how some people thrive, we should spend more time looking *around* them–at such things as their family, their birthplace, or even their birth date. And in revealing that hidden logic, Gladwell presents a fascinating and provocative blueprint for making the most of human potential. (Amazon)

PERSONALITY ASSESSMENTS

In the chapter on Find (and know) Yourself, we talked about personal inventory assessments. Some of them are:

Myers-Briggs Type Indicator (MBTI), DiSC Profile and Holland's Interest Inventory.

COACHING, KEYNOTE ADDRESSES, SEMINARS AND WORKSHOPS

If you need personal interaction, try the Just Do Your Dream Facebook Community or personal one-on-one coaching sessions with the authors. As certified results and life coaches, we offer coaching sessions to help you stay focused and on purpose.

We're also available for group workshops, seminars and keynote addresses.

Your dream is within and sometimes just a little push (or maybe a lot) is what's needed to help you realize it.

Thank you for your desire to do what you always wanted. We're here to help. Please contact us at JustDoYourDream.com

JUST DO YOUR DREAM!

ACKNOWLEDGMENTS

I STARTED this project six years ago. It began with a Visibility Marketing Inc. ten-year anniversary celebration in 2010, then morphed into something much more. Along the way I lost my mother, my rock, the one person whose smile and encouraging words I will miss when this book is published. Her passing set this project back, almost extinguishing it. However, I know that had I given up, it would have disappointed her. I can hear her now: "I didn't raise a quitter."

There are so many people who have helped me along my journey. They contributed in ways in which they may not even know. When I told them what I was doing, just to hear them say, "That's great. I can't wait to read it," was enough encouragement for me to not lose hope and see it to the end.

"On Christ the Solid Rock I stand, all other ground is sinking sand..."

Those are the words to a song we used to sing in church and to Him I owe it all.

July 5, 1997 is the day I gave my heart and pronounced my undying love to Todd Q. Adams. Thank you for being you and always encouraging me to be me. I could not have done this without your love and support. I love you.

Dad, thank you for showing me what fortitude really is. Your courage, vision and business acumen was the light that guided me along this journey. I love and appreciate you.

Tadj and Najah, Mommy loves you. Thank you for supporting me and always asking, "Is the book finished yet?" When the journey became weary, you inspired me to just keep swimming…swimming… swimming…

Dr. Angela Ali, you are poised for greatness. Thank you for supporting me and this project. This book would not be what it has become without your wisdom and contribution.

Cynthia Gilchrist, what can I say? My love and admiration for you goes back to the days of elementary school non-stop giggling. Thank you for believing.

Tonia Gustafson, I've always admired your brilliance, Sis. Thank you for your honesty. One day I will beat you at Words with Friends.

Sharleen Rucker, Terri Rucker Wright, Tina Harrison Rucker, Thea Harris, Karis, Kyle, Jaymin, Skye, Torin, Taylen, Arianna, David, Natessa, Lyra and Kiann. It's all about family. I love you all.

My Sistah Friends, thank you for helping me along this journey. Much love!

Kelly McIntosh, you are the best! Thank you for making this project much better.

Kathy Kovacic, we clicked the day you walked into my office. Thanks for not only being a great designer, but a wonderful friend.

J. Everett Prewitt, I have always looked up to you. Your wisdom and guidance along this process and throughout the years is unmeasurable.

Richard Johnson, thank you for believing in me. It was my pleasure to serve *Kaleidoscope* magazine over 20 years as its writer, Managing Editor and Editor-In-Chief.

Many thanks to everyone profiled in this book and on **JustDoYourDream.com.** This book could not happen without your contributions and belief in this project. All of you have stories to tell which give hope to those who read them. Please continue to inspire and encourage others to Just Do Your Dream!

ABOUT THE AUTHORS

Montrie Rucker Adams,
APR, DTM, MBA

AFTER spending time at her father's chemical business in Puerto Rico and her uncle's cleaners in Cleveland, OH, Montrie Rucker Adams finally fulfilled her dream of entrepreneurship in April, 2000. In 2010, Visibility Marketing Inc. proudly celebrated 10 years of "making people, places and products more visible" with their Don't Drop the Dream celebration.

The milestone prompted the desire to think of other unfulfilled dreams. Believing Walt Disney's, "All our dreams can come true if we have the courage to pursue them," Montrie set out to do what she always wanted- knowing that if we, "Trust in the Lord, He will give us the desires of our heart."

Montrie has won several writing, business and community service awards. She is leading clients, through Visibility Marketing Inc., on the path of Smart Inclusion, a sustainable business practice that includes the skills and talents of all employees.

A certified Results Coach, Montrie helps others realize their dreams by encouraging them to identify their desires and stay focused on achieving them.

A native Clevelander and former fitness instructor, Adams enjoys challenging herself to greater potential, physical fitness, writing, travelling, the theater (performing and spectating) and creative, public speaking.

Montrie is working to spur a *Just Do Your Dream!* movement which is a community helping one another to finally live their dreams. The book, *Just Do Your Dream!, A 7-Step Guide to Help You Do What You Always Wanted* *with stories that Enlighten, Encourage and Inspire,* wiil spur its readers to action.

Married to Todd Q. Adams, she relishes in watching their daughter twirl the baton and son rule on the tennis court.

Angela Adams Ali, Counselor, PhD, LCPC, MFT, BCC

D R. Ali is a psychologist, clinical therapist, and board-certified coach with a private practice in Chicago. She specializes in the research and psychotherapeutic treatment of individuals, couples, and families. Dr. Ali's approach is to empower her clients in ways that improve their insights and help them to embrace healthier realities and relationships.

Prior to Dr. Ali's career as a psychologist, she spent several years in corporate America in the areas of finance and operations. She is also an entrepreneur, and coaches others on how to achieve personal and business goals.

Dr. Ali enjoys reading, exploring new ideas, traveling, neo-soul music, and spending time with those dear to her.

NOTES

Made in the USA
Lexington, KY
14 June 2017